A Guide's Guide to
FLY-FISHING MISTAKES

A Guide's Guide to
FLY-FISHING MISTAKES
Common Problems and How to Correct Them

BY SARA LOW

Illustrations by Rod Walinchus

Skyhorse Publishing

Copyright © 2013 by Sara Low
Illustrations copyright © 2013 by Rod Walinchus
Second paperback edition 2016

Skyhorse Publishing books may be purchased in bulk at special discounts for sales promotion, corporate gifts, fund-raising, or educational purposes. Special editions can also be created to specifications. For details, contact the Special Sales Department, Skyhorse Publishing, 307 West 36th Street, 11th Floor, New York, NY 10018 or info@skyhorsepublishing.com.

Skyhorse® and Skyhorse Publishing® are registered trademarks of Skyhorse Publishing, Inc.®, a Delaware corporation.

Visit our website at www.skyhorsepublishing.com.

10 9 8 7 6 5 4 3 2

Library of Congress Cataloging-in-Publication Data

Low, Sara.
  A guide's guide to flyfishing mistakes : common problems and how to correct them / by Sara Low.
    pages cm
  Includes index.
  ISBN 978-1-62087-598-8 (alk. paper)
  1. Fly fishing--Handbooks, manuals, etc. I. Title. II. Title: Guide's guide to fly fishing mistakes.
  SH456.L69 2013
  799.12'4--dc23
                              2013002676

Cover design by Brian Peterson
Cover photo credit: Dale C. Spartas

Print ISBN: 978-1-5107-1433-5
Ebook ISBN: 978-1-62636-281-9

Printed in China

For my Uncle Freddy, who gave me Long Pond

To fish fine, and far off, is the first and principal rule
for trout-angling.

Charles Cotton, The Compleat Angler, Part II (1676)

CONTENTS

FOREWORD

In *A Guide's Guide to Fly-Fishing Mistakes*, Sara Low speaks to her readers with the voice of experience from hundreds, perhaps thousands, of hours spent on trout water with fishing clients. Her sixteen-plus-year career as a New York licensed guide has placed her in the unique position of literally having seen it all from the mistakes her anglers make with casting, fly movement, presentation, rigging, and a plethora of other technical aspects to the subtlest aquatic insect behavior that needs to be recognized and reckoned with by the discriminating angler who hopes to catch fish, which I believe I'm safe in saying is all of us.

Many people call themselves flyfishers or flyfishermen but most are not able to distinguish between a good drift and a great drift. In her book, Sara makes her readers better anglers by teaching them to be more observant, more critical, and more demanding of themselves. It's one thing to know that something isn't quite right, but quite another to know what it is that needs to be corrected and perhaps more importantly what to do to correct it.

But this book is not only about casting and fishing techniques. There are chapters on stream etiquette, how to dress for changes in weather and season, care of tackle and gear, being safe on the water and so many other aspects of fly fishing which are important for all anglers to be mindful of.

A Guide's Guide to Fly-Fishing Mistakes should be prerequisite reading for any new or fairly new fly fisherman. It basic and at the same time technical and will be a go-to reference book for all angling skill levels.

Cathy Beck
Author, photographer, and trip host
at barryandcathybeck.com

INTRODUCTION

This book provides the opportunity for me to point out adjustments that anglers can make to improve their fly fishing. When guiding an experienced fly fisher, I usually restrict myself to a minimal number of comments. Most skilled anglers hire a guide to find fish, not to teach a clinic. Even so, I observe, sometimes biting my tongue to keep from giving just one more fishing tip.

What I have noticed are the common mistakes shared by many proficient anglers—from those who have been fishing their entire lifetimes to those who picked up a fly rod only recently and took to it naturally. Although written for anglers with experience, my observations should also be of help to new fly fishers who have not had time to develop bad habits.

A Guide's Guide to Fly-Fishing Mistakes has been separated into topics. Each topic's section opens with a tale of a day on the water that illustrates a problem associated with the particular topic. These stories belong to more than one angler on the stream and could have been written about a number of fly fishers. Each anecdote is followed by a common mistake, one that fits the wading boots of many anglers today. The fix for each mistake is a correction I often make—gently, of course. Also included are additional errors and the corrections suggested for them. You will find "Guide Tips," sometimes providing a true *ah-ha!* moment, sometimes not more than a couple of lines on a simple way to solve a typical problem.

Clad in waders and boots, vests, and hats, anglers tend to look alike and, no surprise, so do many of their mistakes. Look up and down a river and you will see what a guide sees. Guides pay attention to the cast of a rod, the position of a line on the water, the drift of a fly. We also notice the joy in every person who comes to the water with a fly rod in hand. This book is meant to expand that joy.

Sara Low
July 12, 2012

A Guide's Guide to
FLY-FISHING MISTAKES

CHAPTER 1

THE RIGHT ROD

An angler walked into a fly shop and looked around. He found a rod in the sale bin: a basic 9-weight rod for general saltwater fishing. Although he had fished in fresh water for years, the angler had never fished in salt water with a fly. He zipped open the case and drew the rod sections out to check their condition. Satisfied, he bought the rod, anticipating he would have use for it one day.

What's wrong with this picture? There's nothing wrong with our angler buying a rod from a fly shop, and there's certainly nothing wrong with the fact that he got it on sale. The mistake is that he did not put a reel and line on the rod and cast it. A test casting session would have helped him determine if the rod's action complemented his casting style or if he would feel comfortable casting it over a period of time. Had he put the sections together and wiggled the rod back and forth, he at least would have been able to judge the stiffness or softness of the rod.

The story continues . . .

Perhaps a year later, the angler took his unused rod on a trip to the coast, where he hired a guide in order to learn to fly fish in salt water. Saltwater fly fishing is planned around the tides, so our angler got up early and met his guide on a beach at 4:00 AM for a beautiful morning of fishing. After casting and retrieving a Lefty's Deceiver fly in the surf for forty minutes, the angler followed his guide onto a stone jetty for another hour of casting and retrieving. Next, they moved to an estuary with a narrow neck that striped bass were known to pass through. An hour later, the angler and his guide moved again. Finally, after scrambling over large slippery boulders, they positioned themselves just above the water, facing the ocean. The angler began casting and retrieving as the guide had taught him. After a while, the angler asked his guide if he could tie on an unweighted fly. He explained that he was accustomed to fishing for hours at a time, but with small flies in freshwater, and that he simply couldn't lift his arm once more to cast the heavy saltwater fly. The guide smiled and pointed out that the fly was not weighted, although it was much larger than a typical freshwater fly. Instead, the guide handed his spare rod to the angler and told him to try casting with it. It was lighter and had a softer action than the angler's rod. The angler relaxed. His arm felt better immediately. Although still sore, he was able to cast and retrieve the Deceiver for the rest of the morning.

The original rod that our angler purchased on sale was a good rod. It was a fast-action rod, and would have worked well in the hands of an angler experienced with its taper. Cast by someone with a technique suited to a different design and a lighter rod, however, the saltwater rod was not such a good deal, even at a great sale price.

A COMMON MISTAKE

The majority of anglers I take on the water bring rods that are not suited to their casting style. A fly fisher may become comfortable with any rod over time, but may not benefit completely from its features. When a casting style does not mesh with the taper or build of a rod, the angler has to work to compensate for the mismatch.

Many rods are purchased for the wrong reasons: recommendations from other anglers, new technology, the right price. There is a range of fly rods to choose from at almost every price point and material. The right rod is the one that best suits the angler's casting style and, of course, fishing plans.

THE FIX

Before buying a new rod, cast it with a reel and properly weighted line. Even better, cast several rods for comparison.

You don't need to be on the water to do this, either. Most fly shops will let you cast on their lawns or in a nearby park. If this isn't possible, find a different supplier. It would be ideal to borrow a rod and use it before making a purchase. Appeal to the friend who told you about the rod of interest, your local fly shop, or a fishing guide. Fly-fishing trade shows offer opportunities for comparing rods and other gear, with a number of rod sellers eager for anglers to try their products.

Before buying a rod, cast several for comparison.

Evaluate a third party's remarks about a rod by considering information about the person making the comments. What is the incentive of the sporting-goods store employee who pushes a particular rod? What is the fishing experience or casting style of an amateur angler who recommends a rod? Is your decision influenced by the marketing instead of the physical qualities of a rod?

ROD SELECTION

The factors that affect your gear selection remain the same all year. A fast-action or tip-flex rod is a stiffer rod. It will cast large streamers, heavily weighted nymphs, even wets. It will cut through a breeze and play large, aggressive fish on heavier weight lines and leaders. But if you are fishing smaller dry flies or nymphs on tiny tippets in crystal clear water, you will want a rod that offers a more gentle presentation with a softer action and generous flexibility that will yield to takes on fine tippet. This would be a slow-action or full-flex rod. A medium-action or mid-flex rod shares attributes with both rods without the extremes of either: The action will be strong enough to cast a good distance, even the full line in the hands of a skilled caster, and the flex will be soft enough to fish small flies and light tippet with precision.

If you need help, find a local casting instructor and ask him or her to evaluate your casting style and suggest a rod that will work for you.

As an angler develops his skills and expands his fishing experiences, he will become comfortable using diverse rod tapers in different circumstances. Even so, his preferred rod—the one he would choose over any others—will always be the one that matches his casting style.

GUIDE TIP

The general rule of thumb is to use a short rod in a limited casting space and a longer rod in more open areas. Personal preference, however, should weigh as heavily as common sense. If you like a seven-and-a-half-foot rod, use it. Common sense tells us to cast a nine-foot rod when fishing from a drift boat. Personal preference may dictate that you bring the eight-and-a-half-foot rod instead.

Whatever rod weight and length you choose to fish, make sure you enjoy it. Fly fishing should bring pleasure. With the exception of common courtesy to others (anglers, property owners, and fish), there is absolutely no rule in fly fishing that cannot be broken. Use the rod that makes you happy.

Use the rod that makes you happy. Photo credit: John Bonasera

CHAPTER 2

GETTING READY

Almost everything had been checked off my list in preparation for the morning's fishing. The only thing missing was one of the anglers. Two were geared up and ready to get on the water, scuffing the dirt with their wading boots. The third sport was reviewing items in his vest, oblivious to the impatience behind the smiles of his buddies—or the guide, namely me. As the angler set a new fly box on the trunk of the car and began to fill it with flies, I suggested he meet us at the water, a short walk from the parking area. The blue-winged olive hatch would last only a brief time, and I wanted my clients to catch every minute of the frenzy.

Three of us approached the river and entered the water. I positioned both anglers. Leaders straightened and flies tied on, the two anglers stood at the ready, watching for the first emergence of the blue-winged olives. The hatch began on cue with a few insects fluttering on the water's surface, then dozens more until the river was blanketed with mayflies floating downstream like a flotilla of sailboats. And the fish responded. Bursting from the depths of the dark water, rainbow and brown trout rose to the surface, some launching straight out of the water to capture the large, green flies.

The sight of a once-placid river being disturbed by hundreds of trout in an orgy of feeding is a startling phenomenon, one that demands a moment to appreciate. The fly fishermen watched for several seconds in disbelief, gathered their nerves, and began to cast. Soon the two found themselves thigh-deep in a river with fish rising all around, thousands of ephemera floating downstream, hundreds of insects taking flight in every direction, rods pitching back and forth, fly lines cutting through the air, sight obliterated by paper-thin wings fluttering over the water. It was like fishing in a snow globe.

Forty minutes later, the river quieted. There were just a few rises to a dozen or so insects that straggled to the surface, late to the party. I looked up at the bank to see Angler No. 3 appear at the river's edge, outfitted perfectly with all gear securely in place, looking sharp and confident, and ready to fish. But the trout had left the table, sated and exhausted after their feast, slipping back into the depths of the river.

Angler No. 3 breaks the heart of every fishing guide. The angler obviously enjoys fiddling with his gadgets, relaxing, fishing according to his own clock. Perhaps he does not care about a phenomenal hatch. But, for those who do care, there are some simple changes to a routine that may improve a fishing outing. Remember these guidelines, so you won't miss that perfect hatch.

A COMMON MISTAKE

Too many times, I have seen anglers arrive at the water unprepared for the day's outing. Whether fishing equipment is out of order or missing, fly boxes need organizing, or leaders have to be replaced, anglers end up spending too much time sitting by their cars when they could be standing in the stream. And as they watch other fishermen suit up and head to the water, the anglers left behind worry about being crowded out of a favorite spot. Worry turns to panic, which in turn compels the angler to rush. Rushing produces more mistakes: forgotten items, stumbles and falls in or out of

An enjoyable part of fishing involves putting gear in order before an outing.

After a season of fishing, fly boxes usually contain a jumble of flies. Organize your flies before getting on the water.

the water, poorly tied knots. Most important, a potentially pleasant day becomes lost in stress.

THE FIX

An enjoyable part of fishing involves putting gear in order: replacing a frayed fishing line, tying on a new leader, straightening fly boxes, replenishing floatant, toying with gadgets. Instead of waiting until just before getting on the stream, build time into your off-water schedule to do the prep work, whether days in advance of fishing or the night before. The time spent in preparation extends the fishing outing and is a valuable way to avoid leaving something behind.

PACKING GEAR

Check the rods and reels you're planning to take on a trip. There is nothing more frustrating than opening an empty rod case when you are steps away from the river or discovering that a heavy saltwater reel was packed alongside a lightweight trout rod. I've seen every variation of this oversight, which can cut short an otherwise well-planned fishing day. Just open each case and look inside before packing the gear.

Take the time to check your waders and boots. Fix or replace the waders that leaked the last time you fished. If you have two or more pairs of wading boots, make sure you are packing a matching pair.

Don't be like the woman who brought a reel with no fly line, or the guy who had a line, but no leader.

As long as there is a fly shop nearby or you are fishing with a guide, most of these mistakes can be corrected. But corrections can keep you off the water, often at an unexpected cost.

FISHING CONDITIONS

Trip preparations include more than just packing gear. Just as important is checking the water conditions and weather forecast for your fishing destination.

A few years ago, I ran into a group of anglers who had travelled from New Jersey to fish New York's Catskill rivers for the weekend. Unfortunately, the rivers were at flood levels. While I was scouting the Beaverkill, hoping to find fishable areas for a client booked for two days later, an angler worked his way out of the river and approached me, asking if the current was always so strong. The group had no idea they were fishing in extreme water levels. Not only was the experience unpleasant for them, it was also very dangerous.

Even two days later, instead of fishing the main river, I was forced to take my client to small feeder streams to fish safely and comfortably.

Many local fly shops list current river conditions on their websites.

The United States Geological Survey (USGS) site provides information updated hourly on the flow of many rivers in the country. And weather reports are available everywhere, from websites to cable television channels devoted to weather. Consult these resources before taking a trip to the stream. They may make you rethink your trip and will help you decide what equipment and clothing to take.

Take pleasure in properly preparing for a fly-fishing trip. The result will be more quality time on the water.

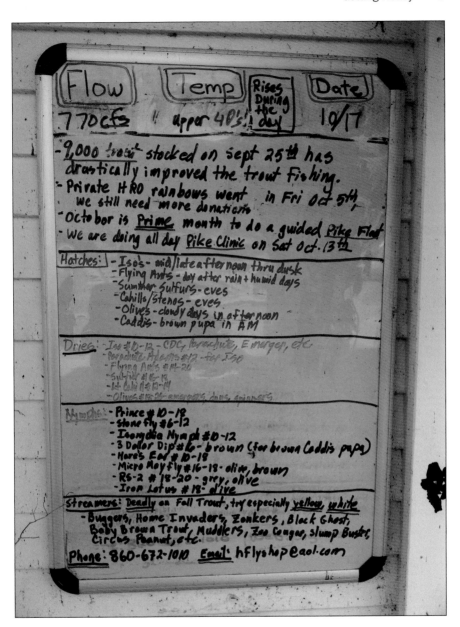

Housatonic River Outfitters lists river conditions on the hatch board outside the shop in Cornwall Bridge, Connecticut. Photo credit: Keith Godfrey

CHAPTER 3

AT THE WATER'S EDGE

everal cars pulled into the anglers' parking lot at the same time. Men poured out of every door. Laughing and joking, they donned waders and fishing vests and assembled fly rods. Car doors slammed shut and teasing subsided as the race began. Half a dozen fly fishermen began to jog down dirt paths to the river in a silent competition to reach the water, step into the prime fishing spot, and cast and hook a trout before the others. Every action was part of the routine that this particular group of anglers goes through on the same stream every week during the fishing season, every

It is unbelievable how difficult it is to see three feet of a slim fishing rod when it is nestled among grasses, leaves, branches, even dirt.

move part of the tradition, even the banter repeated each time. Everything was proceeding according to custom until a shout from one of the anglers stopped everyone. "Don't move," he cried. "Watch where you are stepping." He had lost his rod tip somewhere in the brush. Slowly, each angler began to search for the thirty-two-inch section of the rod. Instead of wading through the water, the anglers were combing through bushes and vines. Back and forth from the water to the cars, six pairs of eyes scanned for the elusive tip. It was never found.

One angler's day was ruined, and five of his buddies were feeling glum.

A COMMON MISTAKE

In anticipation of fishing, an excited angler in a rush does not always secure his gear properly: Rod sections are not tamped down, reels are not seated securely, or vest pockets are not closed. At the end of the day, fatigued fly fishers cut out a few steps and break down equipment even while tramping through the woods. Rod tips, reels, and fly boxes are lost.

I have been a member of too many search parties looking for rod sections lost on the way to the river or on the return. The gatehouse of the Connetquot River State Park on Long Island in New York keeps a modest collection of rod tips discovered in the bushes by the riverkeeper. The collection is modest because most of the lost tips are never found. I have my own collection of fly-fishing gear picked up along riverbanks.

THE FIX

String up your rod, tie a fly on your line, and hook it to the hook keep before you begin your walk to the river.

The fly you tie on may not be the one you plan to fish with, but it will be the one that saves your rod tip.

It is unbelievable how difficult it is to see three feet of a slim fishing rod when it is nestled among grasses, leaves, branches, even dirt.

Don't worry about taking the time to choose the right fly. Do that on the water.

Do take the time to tie one on though. That extra knot you tie will take a lot less time than walking back and forth on a wooded path from your car to the water's edge—however many laps it takes.

String up your rod, tie a fly on your line, and hook it to the hook keep to protect your rod tip from getting lost in the brush when you walk to the water.

Take the precaution so you can begin to fish when you get to the water instead of turning around to retrace your steps.

WALKING TO THE WATER

Rod Tip Forward or Behind?

There are two schools of thought on how to carry a fly rod. Most people favor carrying the rod with its tip pointing in front of them. Believers of this method explain that, with the tip forward, you can watch the rod, ensuring that it does not get hung up on branches or brush. And even if it does, you

GUIDE TIP

An easy way to string a rod is to pull several feet of the fly line off the reel, not counting the leader. Double the end of the line back on itself, creating a small loop near the connection between the fly line and the leader. Hold the two sides of the loop together between the forefinger and thumb. Grasp the rod by the grip, and hold the rod parallel to the ground with the reel facing up. Thread the fly line through the guides as far as you can reach comfortably. It is easy to slide the fly line along the top face of the rod and through the guides in a continuous motion. Next, position the grip of the rod on a flat rock, log, patch of grass, or even the open tailgate of your car. Keep the reel face up. Continue to pass the fly line through the remaining guides, walking to the tip of the rod as you thread rather than bending the rod tip down to you.

Hold the loop between forefinger and thumb.

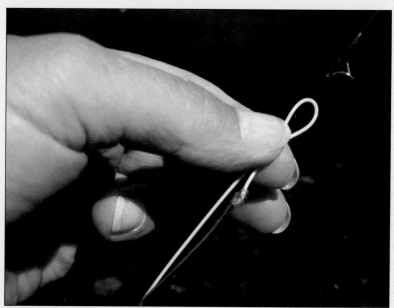

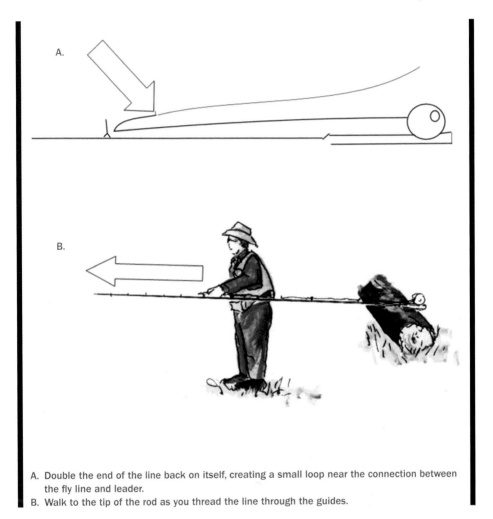

A. Double the end of the line back on itself, creating a small loop near the connection between the fly line and leader.
B. Walk to the tip of the rod as you thread the line through the guides.

can clear the tip easily. With the rod in front of you, you should notice immediately if the rod tip or line gets caught on brush.

There are also advocates for carrying a rod with the tip behind you. The reason for this method is that, if you stumble and fall forward, the rod may drop, but your own forward momentum will not force the tip into the ground, possibly breaking it. A rod pointing behind you can't be walked into something such as a tree and has a better chance of not being snapped. When a rod is carried with the tip behind, it is important that the line is threaded through

Point the rod tip behind you when walking down a slope. If you stumble, the rod tip will not be driven into the ground.

the guides and secured with a fly or in a hand. The secured line helps prevent the top section of the rod from pulling free if snagged on brush.

Whatever your method for carrying a rod, inform the person walking in front of or behind you on a trail and leave plenty of space between you and everyone else as you walk.

The angler in a rush skips details and loses out in the end. Some mishaps are easily corrected, but others can ruin the day. The most everyday errors can be simple oversights that are easily prevented by measuring each step and tallying a checklist, mental or physical.

Fly fishing is all about details: the appropriate fly, a sound cast, a natural drift, and precise timing. The angler who sees to the details in advance preserves both gear and fishing experience.

Zip your pockets to avoid losing gear.

CHAPTER 4

LINE, LEADER, AND TIPPET

A perfect evening: The afternoon sun was cooling on the horizon on a weekday that promised the pool would be empty of anglers except the two of us. My client and I waded into the water ready for an evening spinner fall that typically draws large brown trout to the surface each night for about five days in June. Having waited months for this specific outing, the angler (my client) was prepared with a 5-weight rod, a clean line, and a new leader. As the day darkened, we began to see ovipositing female drakes dipping to the water to release their sacs of eggs. Tremendous brown heads rose to the water's surface to meet the insects, and the orgy began. My client cast to rising fish about thirty feet away. He then moved on to rises farther off. But instead of landing his fly on the water, the angler cast it back and forth in the air, false casting with a vengeance. An accomplished angler, my client was struggling with his forty-foot cast. The line jerked back and forth as he contorted his body to lengthen the cast. "I'm working too hard and can't get the line to move," he said. "I don't understand. Favorite rod, clean line, what is the problem?" he panted. After another minute of watching his efforts, I took the rod and tried it for myself. It was the line. The angler had grabbed a reel loaded with a 4-weight flyline to use on his 5-weight rod. We returned to the car to replace the reel with one holding a 5-weight line and made it back to the water with enough minutes of light left to see a twenty-two-inch brown trout netted after a fifty-five-foot cast.

This is a universal story that can be told of every body of water, every season, and almost every angler. It always takes a few minutes for the fly angler to identify the problem. When the rod does not cast smoothly and the line does not sing out as expected, most anglers blame the situation on a dirty line, rod sections not aligned, the casting stroke—a myriad of excuses. It's a simple fix if the proper fly line is nearby. Otherwise, the mix-up

A good-size brown trout: The result of a well-cast line from a properly balanced rod, reel, and line.

becomes a hindrance, especially if the fish are feeding beyond the distance of a short cast.

A COMMON MISTAKE

The angler who is busy changing flies often loses track of the length of his leader. Whether he continues to lose them to the jaws of fish or has seen too many refusals and not enough takes, the angler who ties on new flies is shortening his leader with each new knot.

It is easy when preoccupied with fly selection to forget about the length of the leader. All too often an angler discovers that he has been fishing with a leader that has been shortened over the course of the day by a succession of snips and new knots for each fly tied on.

Until he lengthens his leader and attaches the last series of flies, testing them one by one, the angler will never know if he had selected the right fly earlier, but turned off the fish because it was tied on to a stumpy leader.

THE FIX

The obvious comment is that fly fishers need to keep track of the amount of tippet and eventually leader that gets cut off when flies are changed. But that does nothing to trigger an inspection of the line, especially when an angler is in a hurry to attach a fly while fish are feeding actively.

A good way to keep track of the length of a leader—especially for those who use knotless tapered leaders—is to add a couple of feet of tippet to the end of the leader. Keep spools of various sizes of tippet in your vest. When you attach a new leader to your line, tie on an additional twenty inches of the corresponding size tippet, such as adding twenty inches of 5x tippet to the end of your 5x leader. When you are fishing and changing flies, you will eventually get to the knot that connects the tippet extension. Don't cut off the knot to tie on a new fly. Instead, attach a new length of tippet, and then tie on your fly.

THE FLY LINE'S CONNECTED TO THE . . .

Elements should correspond in weight, size, or function to the other features of the tackle. The weight of the rod determines the weight of the fly line. The line weight prescribes the size of the reel to be used. Let's review each element of the fly line.

Leaders and Tippet

If you build your own leaders, you will have worked out your preferred system for sizing the length of each section. If you buy tapered leaders, it's a simple matter to pull a new one out of the packet and tie it onto your line. Even those who buy leaders, rather than build them, make decisions based on preference, like whether to attach the leader to the fly line with a knot or with a loop-to-loop connection. Whereas the loop-to-loop speeds the connecting procedure and makes it easier to replace a leader, a knot is a smoother, less obtrusive connection—an important factor when it's drifting in clear water or being reeled in through the rod's guides. I prefer to connect my leader to the fly line with a nail knot.

A. (Elements of fly line and unknotted tapered leader from left to right) Tippet, leader, fly line.

B. (Elements of fly line and knotted tapered leader from left to right) Tippet (smallest diameter), leader midsection (very small diameter), leader midsection (small diameter), leader midsection (thicker diameter), butt section (thickest leader diameter), fly line.

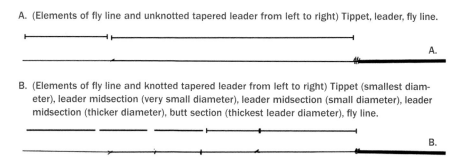

Tippet Size

To determine what size tippet one needs for a particular fly, estimate the size of the fly, divide the number by three, and tie on that size tippet. For example, if you think you are looking at a size 18 Blue-Winged Olive, divide 18 by three, and tie on a 6x tippet.

If the tippet size is too large, the fly will drift awkwardly and not give the lifelike imitation you seek. Conversely, if the size is too small, the tippet will become twisted and kinked during casting.

This weakens the tippet and may result in its breaking just as a fish hits your fly.

That said, when fishing in clear water or a slow current, divide the fly size by four, and drop the size of your tippet accordingly.

A tippet that is too small for the fly will become twisted and weaken during casting.

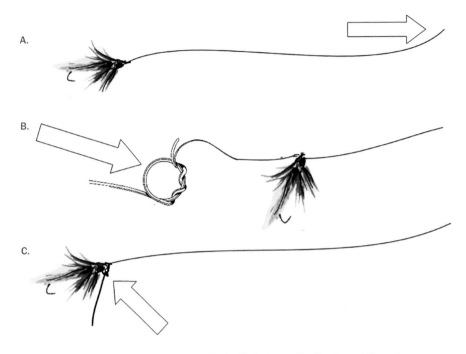

A. Thread a heavy fly onto light tippet, with the fly facing up the line toward the rod.
B. Attach a section of heavy tippet to the light tippet with a surgeon's knot.
C. Make sure the knot is large enough to hold the fly, even with a fish on the hook.

GUIDE TIP

To prevent a heavy fly twisting on a light tippet, thread the tippet through the eye of the hook, so that the fly is facing up the line toward the rod. Then, attach a four-inch piece of 2x or 3x tippet onto the end of the light tippet with a surgeon's knot. Trim the knot. Slide your fly down to the end of the heavy tippet, snug against the surgeon's knot. Make sure that the knot is large enough to stop the fly from sliding off the line, even when pulled by a fish. You will notice that the fly spins freely around the tippet without causing it to curl. Using this rig, you can attach a large or bushy fly on a small diameter tippet that is barely visible in the water.

ADJUST YOUR DRAG

Return to the other end of the fly line to fine-tune the drag system on the reel. It is the rare angler who adjusts the reel's drag during the course of a fishing day.

The drag system allows you to keep constant pressure on a fish being played. Many reels have adjustable drag systems. The drag level may be changed, often with the turn of a knob, from very light to very tight. A light drag allows the line to slip off the spool with little friction, and a tight drag requires strong force to pull the line off the spool.

The drag setting should be adjusted to match the strength of your line, leader, and tippet. If you are fishing for large fish with a heavy fly line and large-size tippet, you will use a heavier drag. Conversely, as you move to lighter lines and smaller tippets, you will ease your drag accordingly. Too much drag, and a strong resistance to the pull of a fish can end in the snapping of tippet, leader, or—in extreme cases—a fly line.

Another factor that should affect the setting of a reel's drag is the stiffness of the fly rod. Fast-action rods, which are usually stiff, do not give or bend as easily when you set a hook or play a fish. If you are using a stiff rod, reduce the reel's drag so that the line can be pulled off the reel by the fish with less resistance. If the rod does not flex and the line is held tight, a burst of energy from a fish can cause the tippet to stretch to its fullest and then break.

Too many fish have been lost because of the incorrect setting of the reel's drag.

GUIDE TIP

Start with a light drag setting on the reel. The setting can always be adjusted, even while playing a fish.

When a fish first makes a run with your fly in its mouth, lower the rod tip to the water. This eases the drag and helps prevent the leader from breaking if the drag setting is tight. Keeping the rod tip high in the air with a significant bend in the rod results in the maximum resistance, which increases the chances for something to break.

Make a point of checking the drag when you begin to fish and each time you tie on a new fly or tippet.

At the end of the day, ease the tension of the drag to preserve the drag system when storing your reel.

THE WEAKEST LINK: KNOTS

In this age of machine-tested equipment, the weakest link from the angler to the fish is often a simple hand-tied connection, a knot. Knots are used at each end of the fly line: one end attaching it to the reel, the other to the leader. They connect lengths of leader tapering to a fly and even a dropper or second fly. Different types of knots are suggested for the various connections. Each knot is usually rated for strength, which holds true if the knot is tied properly.

I have found that even the most seasoned anglers enjoy sitting around sharing tips on knots and, in the early days of the fishing season, practicing tying. But, I've also seen many anglers who do not indulge in this custom and, after a hasty review, if one at all, take to the water with expensive equipment held together by inferior knots.

The most common mistakes made when tying knots occur during the tightening or seating of the knot. A couple of important things to keep in mind:

- When securing a knot, pull slowly to avoid friction that will heat and weaken the monofilament. Monofilament that has been overheated

A well-executed knot will result in a straight monofilament with full strength.

When a knot is being tied, friction will weaken the monofilament and often cause it to curl.

A pig's tail or corkscrew at the end of a tippet indicates that the knot slipped, causing the fly to be lost.

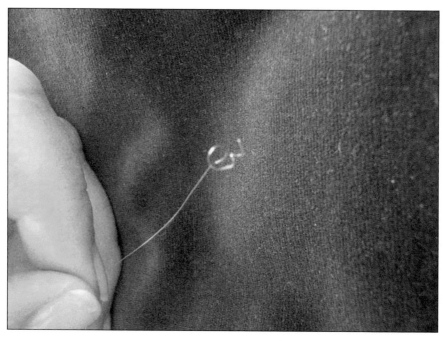

GUIDE TIP

When attaching tippet to a leader, you can skip one size of tippet from 1x to 5x. Your tippet extensions might then be 1x, 3x, and 5x or 2x, 4x, and 5x. After 5x, tippet must be added in one-size steps. If you plan to fish with 7x tippet, add a length of 6x tippet to your 5x tippet, and tie on the 7x tippet after that.

through knot tying becomes curly or wavy and will not sit straight on the water.

- It is common to lubricate the line being tied to seat the knot completely. Wet the line by dipping it in the water or spitting on it. Never put a wet line in your mouth, or you are taking chances with bacteria in the water.
- The telltale sign of a faulty knot after it has slipped is a tight corkscrew curl, often referred to as a pig's tail. After a fly is lost to a fish or snagged in a tree, check the tippet. If the end is straight, the fly broke off cleanly. If the tippet curls like a pig's tail where the knot once was, the fly was lost because the knot slipped.

Count on secure knots to help you land a feisty brown trout. Photo credit: Jeff Ward

CHAPTER 5

APPROACHING THE FISH

A seasoned fisherman came to me one day requesting guide service on the Beaverkill in New York's Catskill Mountains, a river he had fished for many years. He wanted, he said, to approach the water, even his favorite fishing spots, with a new perspective to improve his success at catching fish. And so, he and I spent a day moving up and down a river that the angler had fished almost as long as I'd been walking.

The first thing I noticed each time we stepped into a new pool was that my client, an experienced angler, waded immediately to the obvious spots, choosing to position himself where every angler before and after him would stand. Typically he would settle himself in an area that was protected from the main current, then cast across the fast water to the slower current on the far side. Soon his fly would drag when the section of line drifting in the rapid current pulled the lure that was floating in the distant, slower water. Even after he mended his line or added slack to his line, he was hampered by the fast water flowing between where he was standing and where the fly was drifting. The conditions became even more challenging when the fisherman cast his fly farther away, across more currents of differing speeds.

We entered Barrel Pool, a long stretch with a shallow shelf on the near side that slopes gently down toward a wide, deep gully beyond which lie boulder-strewn shallows by the far bank. The main current runs swiftly through the gully. Large trout are often seen chasing insects to the surface in the shallows on the far side. The great challenge is to cast far enough to reach the big fish while positioning the line with enough slack to allow time for the fly to drift naturally through a fish's range of vision. Unless the water level is low, the length of a cast necessary to reach the fish is too long for most anglers to execute with control. And yet, the fish on that opposite bank are always an enticement.

In the midst of a thick hatch of sulphurs, while my experienced flyfisher worked up a sweat casting over and over again to the far side of the river, I turned to face the shore behind us and, as I'd expected, found fish rising in the shallows we had waded through. Directing my client to this situation, I suggested he cast to the near rises. He scoffed at my direction, exclaiming that these fish were small and not the river monsters found on the far side. After being reminded that his goal was to see the river through fresh eyes, my client begrudgingly began to cast to rises I indicated. To his surprise, he hooked a fifteen-inch rainbow trout that leaped out of the water twice before yielding to the net. After that, he caught a sixteen-inch brown trout, a couple of twelve-inch browns, and finally a nineteen-inch trout that stretched beyond the opening of my net.

The Acid Factory Pool is on the Beaverkill near the town of Horton in New York's Catskill Mountains.

We moved to our last pool of the day—Acid Factory Pool—another long stretch of water that's about ninety feet wide and holds big fish, which rise on the far side of a fast current. My client declared that he wanted to prove to me that he had learned the lessons of reading the river. He would approach the water without guidance first, instead requesting confirmation or corrections after his attempts. The fly angler walked slowly along the rocky shore searching for a telltale rise among the waves and bumpy water. He stopped and, without even wetting his boots, cast his line, letting his fly land not twenty feet across the river and slightly downstream of his position. The fly drifted a couple of feet in the current and was lost in an explosion of water when a monster of a brown trout rose from the dark depths to trap the offering.

This trophy rainbow trout was cruising just off the bank on the Henrys Fork of the Snake River in Idaho.

The smile on the fly fisher's face indicated his joy, but the light in his eyes showed me that he was seeing the river differently. I hope this was the first time for many years to come.

A COMMON MISTAKE

Many anglers rely on techniques and habits that they have developed over years. They are comfortable with their fishing choices and use them for every situation. The angler who prefers to cast downstream, with the river flowing from his right will position himself to fish downstream, with the river flowing from his right, so he can fish at ease regardless of the conditions. Similarly, the angler who is versed in insects may tie on a fly with little regard for what is actually happening in nature, the selection based on his preference or a hatch chart.

THE FIX

We have all heard the line about stopping at the river's edge before stepping in so as to observe what is happening on the water. But, do you really know what it is you are supposed to look for?

If you see a feeding fish, you will probably choose to cast to it. I would and I would recommend this to anyone fishing with me. If you don't see any fish activity, you will have to cast blindly, although you will help your chances of attracting a fish by watching the water for a few minutes, evaluating what you see based on your store of knowledge and common sense.

When you get to the water's edge, before stepping in and wading to a spot that looks comfortable, or casting from an open space on the bank . . . Stop, Look, and Listen.

STOP at the water's edge to gauge what is happening around you. Let the pace of nature influence your actions. You will probably have to slow down.

LOOK at your surroundings and take notice of everything you can see in the water, on top of the water, and above the water.

LISTEN to the sounds of the activity around you, and take note of what you may not be seeing. Can you hear fish breaking the surface of the water?

WHERE TO STAND

Determine where you want to stand in relation to your targeted fish. I usually recommend an angler cast to a fish that is downstream, positioning himself upstream and slightly to the side of the fish. Most of the time, it is easier to achieve a natural drift for the fly from this position by adding slack into the cast.

A great distinction between experienced anglers and those who are truly accomplished is revealed by where the wading fly fisher chooses to stand to fish.

Where do you want to stand, and what are the criteria you use in selecting that spot? Of course, most anglers prefer to stand in a flat-bottomed area that is protected from the full force of a river's current and is a manageable casting distance from feeding fish. Some of these conditions are not as relevant as others.

Let's look at the needs of the fish in comparison to the comfort of the angler.

Protection from the Current

Most often, fish will be found in places that are sheltered from the force of the river's current. Fish expend less energy to rest in these positions. Fish aren't lazy, but do need to forage for every calorie burned. The less energy used, the fewer calories needed, which translates to less food required to stay alive.

An angler planning to fish for more than a few minutes also requires some protection from the current. The angler who is standing in the brunt of a current eventually discovers that his leg muscles will have tensed, a natural reaction to the force and one that drains energy and strength after a period of time. An angler may feel his legs becoming shaky and weakening. For safety and comfort, the angler as well as his prey must seek protection from the current.

Even so, don't go rushing in to a protected spot without first casting to it. If you like the area, chances are that the fish may as well.

Once you have determined your fishing position, you have to get there without disturbing your prey or putting yourself in danger.

WADING

How many times have you either fallen into the water or saved yourself from a dunking? There isn't an angler among us who can't admit to this. You can't help it. A fish is rising or you have not been on the water in a long time. You are looking everywhere for fish or casting as you wade. Instead of concentrating on footing, we multitask by scouting or casting while getting into position.

What seems a minor point while reading in dry clothing becomes very important when an angler is wet and cold and has to stop fishing early to dry off or even avoid hypothermia.

Concentrate on wading. Begin to fish after you have settled in a secure position.

Think about what you are doing as you wade:

- Move slowly.
- Lift your foot just high enough to clear stones or rocks on the riverbed.
- Transfer your body weight completely to one foot before picking up the other.
- Look at the area you are stepping into.
- Always move in a forward direction; don't back up.
- Stop wading before you begin casting.

The majority of falls happen when an angler is just a few feet from the bank. There are a few common causes for tumbles at the water's edge:

- At the end of the day, when an angler moves to leave the water, fatigue causes attention to waver.
- Wading in water that is knee-deep or shallower affects one's balance. In deeper water, a body feels buoyant, but in shallow depths, it becomes top-heavy. It's easier to lose one's balance and topple.
- Closer to the bank, we often look up, taking our eyes off where we are stepping, and then trip on rocks or submerged logs.

OBSERVE THE FISHING AREA AROUND YOU
Note the Weather

Weather conditions should affect your fishing decisions.

Wind blowing across a slow-moving pool usually drives surface-feeding fish down. The wind breaks up the water, making it difficult for fish to watch any insects floating on the surface.

A slight breeze, however, may ruffle the surface gently, breaking the smoothness of a slow pool, but only enough to diminish the fish's visibility. This can be a welcome circumstance for an angler looking for a slight advantage over the naturally honed instincts of a fish.

Pay attention to the direction of the breeze. If you are fishing dry flies, you will want to concentrate your casts to the water near the downwind shore where fish may have chased the emerging insects being blown across the stream.

A bright, sunny day should elicit caution in a fly fisher. An overhead sun will create shadows on the water.

This rainbow was holding tight to the bank. To catch him, the author had to crouch down low and fish from the bank.

The angler may opt to fish from the bank, crouch in the grass, or position himself under overhang to avoid making a shadow on the water.

Rain can affect the water in the same way that wind does. A gentle rain may only break up the surface and cut down on the fish's visibility: another condition that may give the angler an unnatural advantage. A heavy rain usually discourages surface-feeding fish, just as a strong wind will do, forcing them to feed on subsurface insects.

Take Time to Watch the Water Before You Fish

Before you begin to cast, look behind you and above you. The most common cause for frustration and embarrassment among anglers is catching a fly in the brush or a tree on the first back cast. There is no excuse for this. At least be aware of the hazard by turning around to see what is behind you. Assess the entire back cast area, not just up in the air where there may be overhanging branches, but also at the level of your head or lower if you tend to drop your back cast. It's no fun to be caught with your fly in a tree.

Overcome obstacles by choosing a different cast or moving to a less hampered position. Trees, branches, and shrubbery are immobile. An angler is not planted. If possible, inch yourself into the best position that will allow you to cast to your intended prey without catching your line on a branch. If you won't move, consider using a different cast. There are several casts that have been perfected to get around obstructions.

Roll Cast

The first cast most anglers learn is the roll cast, the technique that allows a fly fisher to land a fly on the water without concern for back casts. After learning the roll cast, most anglers move on to more complicated casts in an effort to

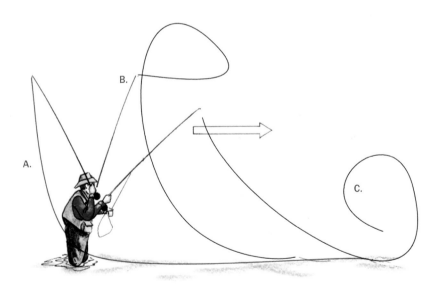

A. Raise your rod slowly to a vertical position until your hand reaches the height of your cheek and the line is bowed behind the rod.
B. Execute a forward cast with a sharp drop of your elbow and hand.
C. The line will roll out on the water like a hoop.

achieve greater casting distance, stronger power strokes, and the sensation of a balletic rhythm on the water.

This is all very natural and satisfying for most of your fishing needs, but, when in trouble, return to your basics. The roll cast should remain in your arsenal of techniques throughout your entire fishing career. This is not a simple cast exclusively for beginners. The roll cast is one of the handiest techniques for fishing many situations. Use it when you find a backdrop of brush close behind you, when you need to bring a sinking line to the surface, and even when you have hooked a submerged or visible log or other obstacle.

To execute the cast, drop your line on the water. Slowly raise your rod to a vertical position (A). At the same time, bring your rod hand to the outside of your shoulder, and raise your hand until your reel is level with your cheek. Angle the rod tip slightly behind your shoulder and pointed away from your body. Stop moving your rod. The line will glide gently in the direction of the rod. Allow the momentum to continue until the line has bowed behind you, creating what looks like a "D" from afar. Execute the forward cast by using your elbow as a pivot point (B). Bring your hand down sharply, and stop at the level of your waist. The fly line will roll on the water like a hoop, ending with the fly landing gently and the line extended straight out from your rod (C).

Aim above the water to straighten your line in the air. Aim directly at your fly to dislodge it from a log. Angle your rod over your head, and cast over the opposite shoulder when the wind is blowing from your casting side.

Continuous Oval Cast

The continuous oval cast, with its nonstop motion, is another option when there is limited room for a back cast. To execute this cast, move your arm in a back-cast motion, but as a sidearm cast about waist level. When your hand swings back to the plane of your body, raise your arm from the shoulder in a slight curving motion until the wrist of your casting hand is at the level of your ear. Without halting the motion, execute a forward cast, leading with your elbow. The fly line will trace the outline of an upside-down "D" by the end of the cast. Basically, your cast will be a straight line back cast at the level of your waist, followed by a semi-circular move to the front.

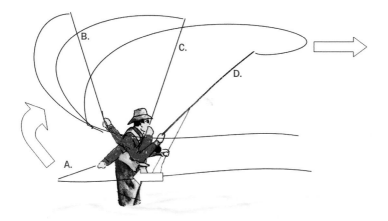

A. Begin side-arm backcast at waist level. Keep backcast level.

B. When your hand reaches your side, curve the cast circling your arm up until your wrist is at ear's height.

C. Without stopping the motion of the cast, begin a forward cast.

D. Stop the forward cast to let the line open up in the air before dropping to water.

Bow-and-Arrow Cast

Casts of twenty-five feet in length or shorter can be accomplished with a bow-and-arrow cast. To shoot the bow-and-arrow cast, strip about fifteen feet of line off the reel and out the end of your rod, letting it fall to the water below your tip. Coil the extra line into a few long loops by draping it over the extended index finger of the hand holding your rod. After completing the coil, transfer the loops to your line hand. The outside coil should lead directly to your rod tip (A). Tighten your grip on the coils, so that if you were to pull your arm down, the rod tip would follow.

In the other hand, hold the rod with your thumb on top of the grip, your elbow pointed down, and your arm in position as if at the end of a cast.

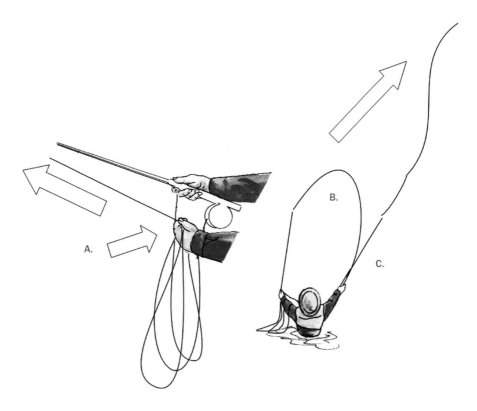

A. Coil fifteen feet of fly line in your line hand. Point the rod tip toward your target.
B. Pull the line hand back until the rod curves into a deep bend.
C. Release the line.

Point the rod in the direction you want to cast your fly. The rod should be fairly parallel to the water, angled slightly up. Bend the rod by pulling the coils in your line hand out to the side (B). The rod should have a deep bend to it.

Let go of the line and the fly (C). Your rod will straighten out, casting the line and dropping the fly gently onto your targeted position.

The bow-and-arrow cast is perfect for streams that require casts of no more than twenty to twenty-five feet in length.

Bow-and-Arrow Cast Position: The rod tip should be bent before the coils are released. Photo credit: Karen Kaplan

CHAPTER 6

IMPROVING YOUR FLY SELECTION

"What about this brown one?" The question was posed by an angler standing sixty feet upstream from me and pointing to his fly box. The angler was a client, one of a group of three experienced fly fishers who were on an annual outing. The trio shared the expense of a guide in order to fish waters they visit infrequently.

Having broken off a fly, the angler was preparing to tie on a new one while I was helping someone else. Not able to look into his fly box, I asked if he had an Isonychia Emerger. "Which is the Isonychia?" he asked. He had picked up flies at a local shop just that morning. Unfamiliar with the large burgundy fly, he asked about a green one, also beyond my sight of vision. When he could not provide a description of the size, he moved on to another brown fly, then a yellow one, a reddish one, and then a black one. "Tie on anything big," I told him. The fish were taking just about anything that was being cast to them. But my angler decided to wait until he could confirm the correct fly of the moment.

A COMMON MISTAKE

Fly fishers successfully hooking fish will shout out the name of the fly luring them in, sharing the information with everyone standing with a rod in his hands. Even anglers who have not hooked into a fish will report on the natural insects they see on the water that may be of interest to fish.

As a guide, I have to be able to recognize insects and match them with flies. Equally important, I must be able to recognize the stage of the life cycle of the insect the fish are keying on. Better versed in this information than the average fly fisher, I am often surprised by the fly suggestions made by anglers on the stream. Sure, there are times when rivalry drives an angler to broad-

A common sight on the water is that of anglers tying on new flies, hoping to match the natural insects.

cast false information, but more often the angler is genuinely trying to share what he sees. Frequently, the interpretation of what an angler sees does not conform to what is really happening.

Reasonably, a fly fisher is familiar with a limited number of aquatic insects and flies. When assessing the insect activity on the water, the angler is influenced by his own knowledge base. But the insect he thinks he sees may not be the one the fish are chasing.

THE FIX

"Match the hatch, match the hatch, match the hatch." This flyfisher's mantra should be repeated whenever you are planning a fishing trip and again when you are staring at the water. The best way to prepare to match a hatch is to know what insects will actually be hatching when you are casting.

HATCHES

Before arriving at the river, arm yourself with information about the aquatic insects that should be active at the time you will be fishing. This information is available online (search "hatch charts" for a pick of websites), at a local fly shop (make sure it's local to the water to be fished), and in printed materials (books, pamphlets, even fishing maps).

The word "hatch" is a bit of a misnomer as most fly fishers use it to refer to the time when an insect emerges from the water, changing from the subsurface phases in its life cycle to the airborne period. In the scientific world, a hatch occurs when the insect emerges from its larval or egg stage, an underwater phenomenon. But, we are fly fishers, so "hatch" is the word.

Determine the fly patterns used to imitate the insects that should be active on the planned fishing day, and supply yourself with a number of each pattern in every stage of the particular insect's life cycle: nymphs, emergers, duns, and spinners for mayflies; nymphs or larvae, pupae and adults for stone-flies, caddis, and midges.

A hatch chart or book can supply you with such detailed information as the hour of day each kind of insect usually emerges from the water. If you fish before that hour, you should use underwater flies that correspond to the insect that will appear on the surface later. If you fish after that hour, you may want to have a supply of the spent spinners which resemble the lifeless insects that have fallen back onto the water.

Hatch charts are general guides based on years of study, but they can't account for weather irregularities in specific years. Early warm weather, extended cold weather, excessive rain, or a dry spell can affect emerging cycles. Local fly shops are the best source for current information, and an angler on the water trumps all other observations on what is happening. Just

Mary Dette and the author in front of the Dette Fly Shop located in Roscoe, New York. The Dettes are one of the last of the original Catskill fly-tying families still producing flies for anglers. Photo credit: Karen Kaplan

because the hatch chart or the fly shop owner suggested a Light Cahill doesn't mean that you should automatically tie one on. If you see a black fly floating down the river, choose a fly that belongs to the corresponding dark family.

WHY THIS FLY

Fish and insect activity will help inform you in your fly selection.

Ask yourself the following questions:

- Is there surface activity from feeding fish?
- Can you see fish activity below the surface?
- Are there insects on the water? Can you identify them? Can you identify the current stage in their life cycles?

Rings on the water indicate that fish are rising to feed on insects at the surface or just below.

- Are there insects flying above the water? Insects flying above the water are not of importance until later when they drop to the water to lay eggs or die. At these times, they interest the fish as food sources.

Fishing at the Surface

Watch the rise—the way a fish comes to the top of the water and takes an insect. Study the telltale signs of the rise to determine where and how the fish is eating, and you will be informed as to what it is eating.

If there are fish rising, look for air bubbles where the fish rose. A bubble is created when a fish takes in air with its prey. A bubble indicates that the insect was on the surface, suggesting that you choose a dry fly: mayfly dun or spinner, adult caddis or stonefly, or terrestrial.

If there are rings but no bubbles, the fish is probably taking insects just under the surface. In this case, tie on an emerger, or swing a wet fly through the water.

GUIDE TIP

When fishing on the surface, start with an emerger instead of a dun or spinner, even with a mass of adult insects floating on the water. Most of the time, the fish are picking off insects as they struggle to break through the film on the surface of the water.

Fishing Under the Surface

When fish are feeding below the surface, visual cues are detectable only when the water is clear and the surface is smooth. Look for shadows of the fish on the bottom of the stream, a puff of sediment blown by the motion of gills, the white of a mouth opening, or the flash of the side of a fish as it rolls to eat a nymph. When you see these signs, tie on a nymph.

GUIDE TIP

If feeding fish continue to refuse your offering, change to a fly that is a size smaller than what you are using.

If this doesn't work, change to a fly that represents a different stage in the life cycle of the insect you are imitating. Go younger. It pays to have several patterns to imitate active nymphs, emergers, and adult insects.

Do your research in advance, and arrive at the water prepared. Take the time streamside to observe fish activity. Identify the visible insects. Select the fly that matches the criteria of the moment, and cast into the water. A tug at the end of your line will never feel so sweet.

Identify the active insects that are visible.

CHAPTER 7

CASTING

Casting practice on a lawn is important, but can drag into tedium after a while. I saw this happening with one of my fly-fishing students last summer, so I asked him to follow me into the middle of the river for a lesson on the water, away from overhanging tree branches and a backdrop of dense brush all stretching out to snag his fly line. We practiced casting until I could see that this was beginning to drag as well, then I tied a fly onto the end of his line for a lesson on presentation and drift. A fast learner, he was soon casting and drifting a dry fly in anticipation of raising his first trout.

We were on the West Branch of the Farmington River in northwest Connecticut, a popular destination with challenging runs and crafty, large

Smooth acceleration creates a forward cast with a clean, open loop. Photo credit: Karen Kaplan

fish. After every cast, the angler whipped his head around and looked over my shoulder. Then, he would pick up his line to recast after allowing time for the fly to settle and drift in the current. Finally, I followed his gaze to a lone fly fisher casting and drifting his fly, just like my guy was doing. Almost. I asked my client what he was looking at. He sighed and replied that the fly fisherman upstream seemed to be surrounded by fish that were rising noisily, while we were standing in a section of the river that appeared empty of life.

Never one to let a lesson pass by unlearned, I turned my client upstream and directed him to watch the other fly fisher and to describe what he saw. My student saw an angler with fish splashing all around him. I saw an angler casting with a perfect rainbow arc made by dropping his rod tip too far on his back cast and letting his line hit the water behind and then again in front of him while false casting. The splashes my client interpreted as rising fish were the popping sounds made each time the line ripped off the water on the back and forward casts. No fish were rising around the angler; chances are no fish would ever rise around the angler while his casts ripped the water.

A fly line will hit the water behind an angler who allows his rod tip to drop beyond vertical on the back cast.

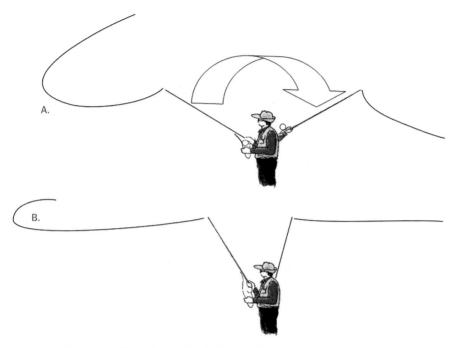

A. Bending the wrist while casting or allowing the rod tip to drop causes a sloppy cast and
compromises line control.
B. Mastering the wrist and rod movement improves a cast and its presentation.

A COMMON MISTAKE

A common casting error is the early acceleration of the casting stroke, which
leads to ripping the fly off the water during the initial back cast. This action
causes guides and accomplished anglers alike to cringe.

Before the initial back cast, the line rests on the water, with the rod tip
pointing to the surface. The error occurs when the angler raises his rod tip

Raise the rod tip slowly to bring the fly line off the water. Once the line is out of the water,
accelerate the speed of your cast.

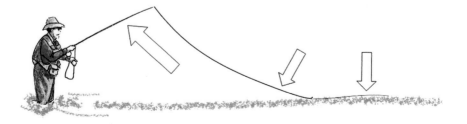

rapidly to initiate the back cast. The water is disturbed as the fly line speeds through it. By the time the fly has left the water, the line has torn through the water with a ripping sound and spoiled the fishing.

THE FIX

The easiest mistake to correct is an angler's timing on the initial back cast. As an angler begins to cast with the line stretched out on the water in front of him, he should raise the rod tip slowly until most of the fly line is above the water, even just an inch. Once the line (but not the leader) is out of the water, the angler should start to accelerate the speed of the cast.

CASTING TECHNIQUES
Line Speed

If I were charged with fixing only one casting problem, I would choose to correct line speed. Line speed, in this case, refers to the rate of acceleration governing the fly line during the cast.

Line speed affects accuracy and distance. An angler who controls the line speed of a cast, controls the presentation of a cast.

Slow line speed will cause a line to sag during the cast. A sagging line has no energy and hinders good presentation and distance in the cast. When the fly line dips in the middle during false casting, hitting the water behind and in front of the angler, energy needs to be introduced into the cast. The angler needs to accelerate his cast with more force before coming to a complete stop and then begin the next stroke as soon as the line has straightened in the air.

At the other end of the spectrum, rapidly whipping the rod back and forth makes the line move too quickly and doesn't give it time to straighten in either direction. If the fly line does not straighten, energy from the rod can't be transferred to the line. The rod and line whip quickly through the air, but energy is never loaded properly into the rod or line, hindering accuracy and distance in the cast. To correct whipping a cast, the angler must bring each cast to a complete stop and allow the fly line to straighten in the air before beginning the next cast.

Let's break casting into manageable segments, as explained by a fishing guide and not a nuclear physicist.

Casting Stroke

Viewed from a distance, casting a fly line appears to be a fluid motion, a continuous, smooth action. Even though there are many techniques to casting a fly rod, they all rest on the same basic rules: acceleration to a stop on the back cast, a pause while the fly line straightens out behind the caster, then acceleration to a stop on the forward cast.

The casting stroke throws the line behind the angler or in front of him, depending on whether it is a back cast or a forward cast. Energy is imparted from the angler to the rod during the casting stroke. The energy is stored in the rod until the stroke stops, the rod straightens out, and the energy is transferred to the fly line.

The more energy in the cast, the more the line moves. The more controlled and smooth the casting motion, the more the angler is able to direct the cast. If increased energy moves the fly line best and skilled casting techniques result in more accurate casting, then an energetic and controlled cast will land the fly where the angler wants it to land.

The forward casting stroke moves the rod 50 degrees from the stopped position of the back cast.

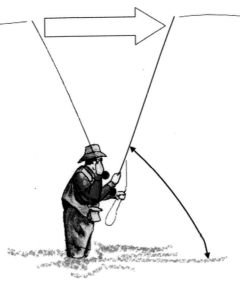

The casting stroke should not allow the rod tip to drop beyond vertical on the back cast. Photo credit: Bert Darrow

Length of the Casting Stroke

Nearly every angler I see would benefit from shortening his casting stroke, by stopping earlier on both the back cast and the forward cast. Unless you are casting a long line, your cast will probably improve with a shorter stroke.

This does not mean you should cramp your stroke or use less arm. It should be a full motion, but the casting stroke should not allow the rod tip to drop beyond vertical on the back cast or the rod to become horizontal to the water on the forward cast.

Watch your back cast to see where your rod hand stops when making the cast. Bring your cast to a complete stop when your thumb reaches your shoulder in a position that is parallel to your upper arm. Whether your casting stroke is moving straight up and down or in a sidearm motion, your thumb should come back only as far as your shoulder. Stop your back cast without bending the wrist, and don't let your thumb move or point behind you. Momentum can force the hand to continue a short distance beyond the intended stopping point, but this motion minimizes the kickback in the spring of the rod tip and should not be resisted. Just let it happen.

The forward cast should mirror the back cast. After the fly line has straightened out behind you on the back cast, begin the forward cast. In the basic cast, with the rod in front of the body, the forward cast should be a motion that drives the elbow straight down. When the elbow is pointing to the water, the forearm completes the stroke by opening to a 50-degree angle, and then stops abruptly. The fly line should unfurl in front of you, straightening its full length in the air. If another false cast is needed, begin the back-cast stroke only after the line has extended completely in front of you.

GUIDE TIP

Pull twenty to twenty-five feet of fly line (not counting the leader) off your reel before beginning to cast. Remember that a fly rod works by casting the weight of the line, not the feather at the end of the leader. Line control requires energy to do three things: straighten the line in the air, add length to the line while casting, and to land the fly on target. To impart energy to the rod, a sufficient length of line is needed just to get the cast moving. Without a good length of line out, the angler can continue to false cast the same length line, never developing enough energy in the rod to draw more line or to straighten the line in the air.

Final Cast

Novice and experienced anglers alike often drop their final cast at the end of the stroke instead of bringing the rod to an abrupt stop and allowing the line to straighten out in front before lowering the line to the water.

Subconsciously, we think we can improve a cast by easing the fly to the water gently. The tendency to follow through is natural. We are taught to follow through in just about every other sport: when we swing a golf club, tennis racquet, or baseball bat, when we shoot a hoop, or serve a volleyball. These lessons create muscle memory and make sense for all but the fly fisher. Following through stops acceleration and allows the energy stored in the rod to dissipate. Instead of sending the fly line out straight and sharp, the cast softens and will not reach the target in good form. Accelerate the casting stroke to a complete stop with the rod (for most casts) angled at about 50 degrees above the water.

It is only after the line sails out in front of the angler and straightens horizontally over the water to its full length that the fly rod should be lowered gently, allowing the fly line to fall to the water.

Wrist Action

There are anglers who cast solely by cocking their wrists back and forth. This action, perfected over years, can work, but is not recommended as a casting stroke of choice. If you are a wrist caster, let's try to break you of this habit.

When an angler bends his wrist, he usually snaps it in a way that changes the speed of the line. The motion of cocking the wrist will jerk the rod tip,

A. Snapping the wrist changes the speed of the line, jerking the rod tip and causing a dip or tailing loop in the fly line.
B. Stiff wrists and smooth acceleration of the cast will keep the casting loops open.

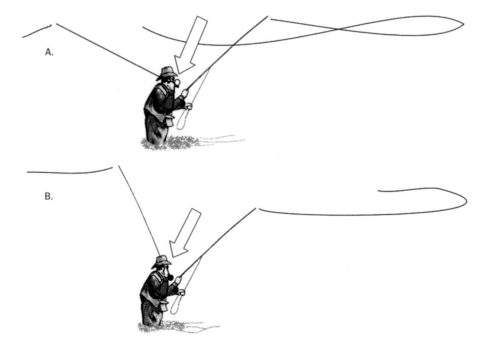

Stop your back cast when your thumb reaches your shoulder in a position that is parallel to your upper arm.

which in turn causes the fly line to follow with a dip or tailing loop. Tailing loops are the most common source of wind knots, bird's nests, and every other tangle that can happen to a leader.

When the wrist is cocked during the back cast, the rod tip points behind the angler at a greater angle than is desired. Because the fly line follows the direction of the rod tip, a rod tip that points down sends the fly line down toward the water. As the line drops to the water in back, the cast loses speed, which translates to a loss of energy. The angler then usually thrashes back and forth trying to cast a line that will not travel far beyond the rod tip. Instead, it's best to start the cast over again, or to pull in line while false casting until there is no sign of a dip in the line. After this, the angler can shoot line on subsequent false casts to attain the length of cast desired.

When you have a problem with a cast, it's really most effective to start the cast over again. This won't tire your casting arm as much as flailing

Don't break the wrist. Stop your back cast without bending the wrist or pointing your thumb behind you.

through the repairs will, and it reduces the chance of slapping the water with dropped casts, which can spook fish.

Snapping the Line

The snap of a fly line zipping through the air is the sign of an error that is obvious even to the guide who is scanning the water and not watching the angler. The resulting sound is just like the crack of a whip. A crack or snapping sound indicates that the angler is starting his next casting stroke too early, not pausing long enough for the fly line to straighten out from the previous cast before beginning the next one. Not only is this sound a source of embarrassment (or should be), but it also indicates that the cast will not perform as intended. There will be a constant loss of energy from the fly rod each time the cast is started prematurely. This will affect the distance and accuracy of the cast. Let the fly line straighten before beginning the next cast; the sound will disappear, and your cast will improve.

False Casting

Many anglers false cast much more than necessary. It's like a lot of talk and no action. A fish can't be caught on a hook that is flying through the air. False casting, the action of back and forward casting without dropping the line to the water, has important utilities. False casting should be used to correct the length of the line being cast: shooting line to lengthen it or pulling in line to shorten it while measuring for distance mid-air over a target.

A short series of false casts is also helpful when changing the direction of a cast. To reposition where the line will land on the water, the angler pivots his body while false casting, This is especially productive when the fly has drifted so far downstream that the fly cannot be repositioned to its upstream target with just a single cast.

A third reason for a false cast is to fling water off a dry fly that has become too wet to float properly.

Lengthen your cast by shooting line out while false casting.

CHAPTER 8

TERMINAL TACKLE

Standing ankle-deep in a cold, cold river in early November, the angler cast to the far side of the main current of a fifty-foot-wide tributary. It was early in the morning, just after dawn, and the water was still dark. A novice to the area, the angler was casting blindly, trusting his guide's experience and knowledge. As the sky brightened, he was able to see into the water and suddenly stepped back, startled. "What are those?" he shouted, referring to the scores of large fish forcing their way upstream inches from his boot. "Why am I casting over there when there are huge fish right here?" "Those are salmon," I replied calmly, adding "And you are fishing for steelhead." "Well, can I fish for the salmon?" he asked. Of course he could fish for the salmon, and he did, but only after we changed his rig by removing the heavy weight on his leader and replacing the fly with another.

Different fishing situations call for different rigging. Proper rigging techniques will result in more successful casting, presentation of flies, and landing of fish.

A COMMON MISTAKE

The fly fisher casting a nymph into the water is counting on the common knowledge that 90 percent of the fish are taken on flies under the surface. Why is it, then, that an angler who is fishing under the surface in a healthy river teeming with trout can be skunked, going home with no strikes?

The answer is usually that the angler hasn't been getting his fly down to the fish, especially in nutrient-rich water that offers lots of food options to fish that will not swim too far for a morsel.

Imagine the body of water you are fishing, from bottom to surface. Each vertical section of the water can be described as a column. Fish feed at different depths of the water column depending on water temperature, insect activity, time of day, and a host of other factors.

Anglers will pore through their fly boxes in search of a choice nymph, tie it on, cast it into the current, perhaps even impart a lifelike drift to it, and wait for a fish to notice the fly. Then they wonder why they are not catching 90 percent of the fish!

THE FIX

To bring a nymph to the fish's mouth, the fly or line must be weighted correctly so as to drift at the appropriate depth in the water column.

If you are uncertain of the depth to be fished, work the water column systematically, continuing to introduce weight. After making several casts and fishing at one depth, attach additional weight to the line and try again, repeating this exercise until the fly attracts a fish or bumps along the bottom.

Before casting a nymph, drop the fly in water close enough so you can observe how far and how quickly the nymph sinks. If the fly is to be fished in moving water with a fast current, it may need extra weight to reach lower depths quickly.

A fly that is not heavy enough to sink to the bottom of the water column can be modified by the addition of extra weight. Add-on weight comes in several forms and measures of heaviness.

To add extra weight, attach it to the tippet six to twelve inches above the fly. Keeping the weight close to the fly ensures that the fly will drift at the same depth as the weight. The free-flowing tippet between the weight and the fly allows the fly to move about realistically in the current.

Different Weights

Split-Shot

In the old days of not-so-long ago, split-shot referred to a little ball formed of lead with a crack running through it. The leader was run through the crack, and the shot was pinched with pliers or teeth, so that it clamped around the leader.

Nowadays, split-shot can be made of non-toxic materials and even come with grips like butterfly wings so they can be opened and used again.

Twist-on Strips

Lead or non-toxic weight that is pliable and cut into small bands can be wrapped around a leader to sink a fly.

Sinking Paste or Putty

Weight can be added to the fly by rubbing a sinking paste on the leader. The paste helps the fly break the surface of the water and slowly sink in depth.

Sinking putty is a soft substance that can be molded by hand and pressed onto the leader.

Special note: The use of lead or extra weight is controlled in some states and protected waters. Consult the state fishing regulations before you pile on the weight.

GUIDE TIP

Try one of these methods to prevent split-shot from slipping on the leader.

• If using removable shot with wings, wrap the tippet through the crack or split twice before pinching the shot closed. Crimp tight.

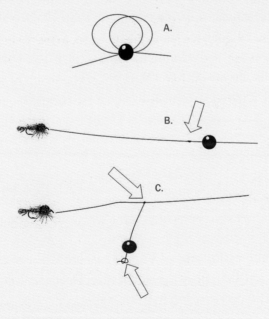

A. Wrap the tippet through the split twice before pinching the shot closed.
B. Attach the weight above a knot tied eight inches from the fly.
C. Attach the weight to the untrimmed tag line of your tippet knot.

- Attach the weight above a knot tied about eight inches above the fly. If you are using a tapered leader, cut off the bottom foot of the tippet section and tie it back on, so you end up with approximately eight inches of tippet below the knot. If you build your own leaders, add an eight-inch extension to your tippet. Tie your fly onto the extension.
- When tying on the tippet, don't trim the knot. Instead, leave a tag measuring six to eight inches in length. Tie an overhand knot at the end of the tag. Attach the extra weights to the tag instead of to the tippet itself. The knot at the end will prevent the weights from sliding off.

ADDING EXTRAS: STRIKE INDICATORS AND DROPPERS

Strike Indicators

Strike indicators come in many shapes and have a few different uses. They can be a length of yarn, a torpedo-shaped plastic float, a gob of buoyant putty, or even a high-floating dry fly. The most common use of a strike indicator is to provide a sign to the angler that a fish has taken a nymph into its mouth. The indicator is also used to suspend a nymph at a particular depth and to gauge whether a submerged fly is dragging in the current.

A regular question asked by anglers is where to position the strike indicator in relation to the fly. The answer depends on how deep you want to drift the nymph. Basically, the strike indicator should be attached above the fly one-and-a-half times the depth the fly is to be fished. If you plan to drift the nymph two feet below the surface, attach the indicator three-and-a-half feet up the leader from the fly. If you want to drag your fly along the bottom of a five-foot-deep river, attach the indicator seven-and-a-half feet above the fly. Don't walk in the water to measure the depth. Just give it your best guess.

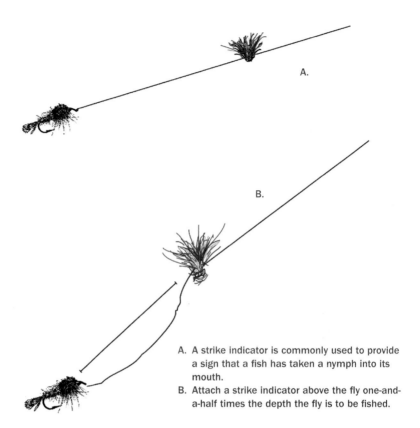

A. A strike indicator is commonly used to provide a sign that a fish has taken a nymph into its mouth.
B. Attach a strike indicator above the fly one-and-a-half times the depth the fly is to be fished.

GUIDE TIP

For fishing at the end of the day or with the smallest of dry flies (when you can see your fly only by squinting), attach a tiny wad of floatant putty to the leader about two feet above the fly. Floatant putty comes in a variety of bright colors. Watch the putty drift downstream. If you notice a rise (even a dimple) within a couple of feet of the fluorescent blob, set the hook. The putty will have to be replaced often because it is easily knocked off a leader when used in small sizes, and it may gum up your leader. But, it's worth the effort. This trick could lengthen your fishing day or curb any hesitation about using tiny flies.

Droppers

Double your fun and increase your chances of attracting a fish by adding a dropper to your rig. A dropper is an additional fly tied on your line to be fished simultaneously with your original fly.

To add a dropper, you can tie a length of tippet to the bend of the hook of your first fly using a clinch knot. Tie the second fly onto the end of the added tippet.

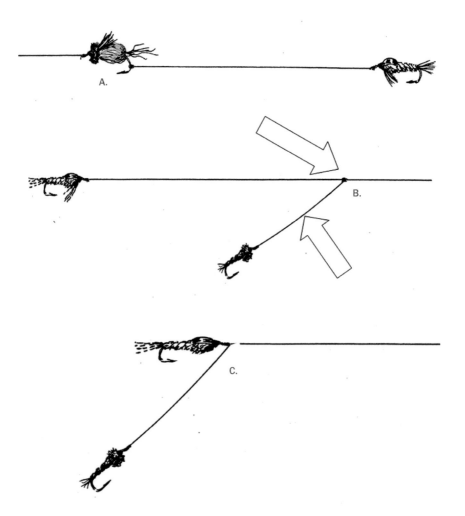

A. Attach a dropper fly to the tippet that is tied to the bend of the hook of your first fly.
B. Tie a fly to the untrimmed tag of the knot attaching the tippet.
C. Attach a dropper to the tippet that is tied to the eye of the hook of your first fly.

Another method used to add a dropper is to run the second tippet through the eye of the first hook, thereby having two clinch knots tied to the nose of your first fly. Unless your dropper is very small and unweighted and your first fly is large, I find this setup problematic as it alters the float of the top fly.

A better alternative is to tie a length of tippet onto your leader leaving a long tag line from the leader at your knot. Instead of snipping off the tag, tie your first fly to it and your trailing fly at the free end of the tippet.

A traditional dropper setup consists of a nymph tied on to a dry fly. The dry fly must be large enough to stay afloat even as the nymph's weight pulls it down. The dry fly acts as a strike indicator and allows the angler to fish above the surface while covering below with the nymph.

GUIDE TIP

If a hatch is in progress, use a nymph and a dry fly from the same insect family to represent the larval and adult stages.

Experiment with your flies. Tie on two dries: the larger size is followed by the smaller. The larger fly may draw fish to the smaller fly. Or add a wet fly to your dry fly to comb the subsurface for emergers. Two different nymphs will test your selection of fly color and silhouette. Tie on a weighted nymph and add an unweighted streamer. You have created your own food chain: a minnow swimming after its dinner! Fish it with a retrieve to impart movement to the streamer. Even if a real fish does not join in the parade, you will have fun. Finally, try two streamers to imitate a dace chasing a minnow. What voracious rainbow would not attack such bold prey?

You can add several droppers to your line, creating a hatch of your own. Your only limitations are the hampering of your cast by the additional weight of the flies and, more importantly, the legal limit to the number of hook points allowed by state fishing regulations.

Whatever rig you create, drift it close to you before fishing, so you can observe the movement of each fly in the water. Try to move the flies with various retrieves to create different action. If you know what movement you want to give your flies, you can fish them more realistically.

CHAPTER 9

LINE PRESENTATION

Three days is a long time for an angler to fish with a guide on a five-mile stretch of river. But, this was the plan, crafted to allow the angler free time to fish a new river while I introduced his son to fly fishing. It was one day into the long weekend, and I could see that the plan was showing cracks. As a novice, the teenager was following instructions and catching fish. The father was testing his memory of fishing lessons learned years before and, unfortunately, his memory had dropped some of the details.

Angler Dad's fly line lifted smoothly off the water as he began his back cast with a stroke that stopped with his thumb pointed directly to the sky: a textbook cast. The line straightened in the air behind him and, with perfect timing, Angler Dad started his forward cast, dropping his elbow, then his forearm, accelerating to a stop when the rod was angled about 50 degrees above the river's surface. I smiled. Some of the signature techniques of his first casting coach were still evident, even after a dozen years: thumb to forehead, drifting the rod at the end of each cast. I could see that Angler Dad had been taught by one of the best.

The casting loop opened in the air into a straight line parallel to the water. My smile deepened at the sight, but dropped in dismay when the line was lowered to the water, landing in a straight line without a break anywhere along its forty-five-foot length. Over and over again, Angler Dad picked up his line and cast in this manner. The aerial segment of the cast was perfect. The perfection was marred by his presentation at the end when he finished the cast in a straight line on the water.

Consistency is an objective when fly casting. Unfortunately, the presentation of this cast was consistently flawed. The fly landed lightly on the water, sitting up as tempting to the fish as the naturals floating down the stream. But, the straight line presentation allowed the fly to be dragged by the pull of the current immediately upon hitting the water. Any imitation of the natural insect was destroyed by the drag.

Gently, I tried to remind Angler Dad of the need to add slack to his downstream presentation. Frustrated by his unrewarded efforts, Angler Dad did not want to hear anything about casting from me. He had learned from Joan Wulff, he barked. Yes, the bones of a Joan Wulff cast were visible, but they were the structure of the basic cast and no longer included the practical stage: the presentation to a fish.

His cast was picture perfect, without question. But, once a caster can control the fly line enough to land it straight, he is taught to present the line for fishing by adding slack or a curve to compensate for the current. Angler Dad forgot about this stage, an important lesson that is taught at the fly casting school. With his final presentation, Angler Dad was ruining his perfect cast. After all, his goal was to hook a fish, not drop a straight line on the water.

A COMMON MISTAKE

Ninety-eight times out of 100, a fish refuses a fly that does not exhibit the natural behavioral characteristics of the insect it is meant to represent. And ninety-eight of those ninety-eight times, the angler is making a mistake in the presentation of the fly to the fish.

The sight of a rising fish often drives common sense from an angler who will wade into the water, stop a comfortable distance from his target, and begin to cast. What angler has not ignored the many currents flowing between him and a rising fish, or even the hint of a fish feeding under the surface?

By not paying attention to the speeds of the different currents in the water, the angler will let his fly drift unnaturally or drag.

Drag occurs when a fly is floating at a speed that differs from the water current it is in. Whether the fly is moving faster or more slowly than the current, it will have drag. A fly will drag if some of the fly line on the water flows in a current that runs at a different speed from the current the fly is in. Visible as a wake following a motorboat, drag is aptly named: It's a drag, and it will turn a fish away from a fly in a nanosecond.

The angler may not be able to discern drag, but a fish can. If you're fishing with a dry fly, compare the speed of your fly to detritus floating in the water next to it. If your fly is moving at a different speed than everything

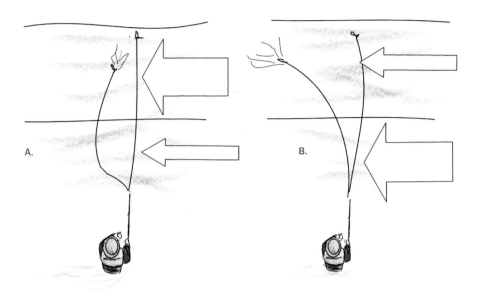

A. If the current pulls a middle section of the line faster than the fly, a downstream belly will drag the fly downstream.
B. If the fly is in the faster current, the line will hinge at the seam between the two currents and slow the drift of the fly.

around it, there is drag. If you are fishing a nymph with a strike indicator, compare the speed of the indicator to debris floating on the water.

Another indication of drag is the belly that appears in the line on the water as it drifts downstream. The belly, or curve, occurs when a section of the fly line is floating in a current that is running at a different speed than the current the fly is in. If the speed of the current pulls a middle section of the line faster than the fly, a downstream curve, or belly, results. The downstream belly will pull on the fly, causing it to move unnaturally fast. If the fly is in the faster current, the line will hinge at the seam between the two currents, causing the fly to swing unnaturally at the end of its drift. In both situations, the fly will drag.

THE FIX

To counter drag, you must throw extra line into your cast. The additional length of line, when it lands on the water, becomes slack. Slack on the water can provide a longer natural and drag-free float.

If too many currents run between you and the fish, you can choose the smart option and move to another position. If this is not possible, there are a few tricks to coax more inches into a drag-free drift for a fly.

SLACK

After learning to cast a fly line perfectly straight, an angler needs to become skilled in adding slack to the presentation. Slack, or extra line on the water, is important when fishing dry flies or nymphs, both of which require a natural, drag-free drift. In the right position, slack will provide more time for the fly to drift with the current before the line and the fly are swept away by the speed of an intervening current.

The angler has many tools for presenting slack into the line to extend the drag-free drift of the fly. Slack can be added and controlled after the fly has landed on the water: an action that is referred to as mending. Slack can also be added at the end of the cast before the line is dropped to the water: a technique referred to as an aerial mend.

MENDING ON THE WATER

The object of a mend is to reposition the line on the water without disturbing or moving the fly. To mend successfully, hold extra line in your line hand. Immediately after casting and dropping your line to the water, flick the rod tip with a circular motion of your arm, simultaneously letting some of the spare line pull out from the line hand.

To execute the mend, work your casting arm as if you were turning a jump rope.

The move must be forceful enough to pick the line off the water and swing it upstream, but controlled enough not to disturb the fly.

In most situations, the added slack should be positioned upstream of the fly to eliminate drag.

Mending Technique

For on-the-water mends, the line and fly must be floating on the water after the completion of a cast.

- Hold the rod with a firm grip, elbow down at your side.
- Move your lower arm in a circle to turn the fly line. This is the jump rope move.

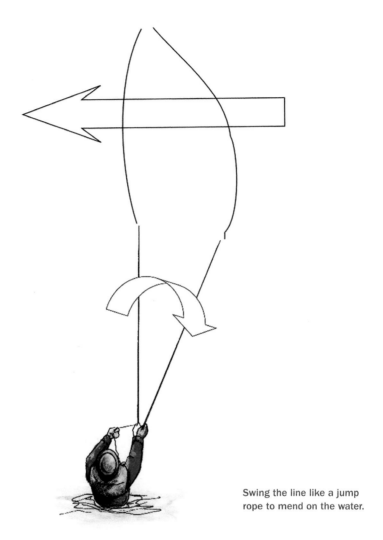

Swing the line like a jump
rope to mend on the water.

•   The circle should move downstream to upstream. The line will swing in
the air, landing on the water in a position upstream of where it started.

To avoid disturbing the fly while mending, it is important to add line.
When the rod tip swings a fixed-length line in a circle for the mend, additional
line will draw either from the length floating on the water or from what is held
in the angler's hand. In preparation for a mend, pull extra line off the reel before
making your cast. Coil the line into several long loops and hold them in your

line hand. While making the circle or jumping rope with the fly line, let additional line be pulled from the excess loops held in your hand.

The basic steps for mending on the water require committed and firm gestures.

GUIDE TIP

Visualize the swinging of a jump rope when you mend your line. It is important to use the circular motion. If the rod tip is moved upstream on a flat plane, without the circle, the fly line will be pulled through the water, disturbing fish as well as the surface of the water and dragging the fly with it.

To mend a long line, it is necessary to swing the line energetically in a larger circle. This action may require rotating the whole arm in the jump rope move. The accomplished mender will apply enough force to move the line without shifting the fly.

A mend works best when it is started immediately after the fly line has landed on the water. The tendency of water to be attracted to other substances—the adhesion quality—makes it difficult to pull a fly line out of the water. Any delay allows time for the line to sink, however slightly. The combined effects of the adhesion quality of water and the sinking of the line hamper the success of the mend.

AERIAL MENDS

By taking advantage of line control in a cast, the angler can position the fly line before it lands on the water with specialty casts. This action is referred to as an aerial mend.

It is usually preferable to mend in the air before the line hits the water instead of after a cast has been completed and the line has settled on the water. An aerial mend involves putting the line and extra slack in position without disturbing the water. By using one of the casts developed to accommodate slack, the angler can better manage the fly line and target the placement on the water of the line in relation to the fly.

The physics of casting teach us that the fly line follows the rod tip during the cast. If the rod tip travels in a straight line, the line being cast will travel in a straight line. If the rod tip drops, the line being cast will also drop. And, if the rod tip is swung in one direction and back to its original position, the line sliding out of the rod tip at the time will also shift to the new direction and back to its original position. This is the principle that gives us a number of different casts for aerial mends.

Reach Cast

The reach cast is used to control the position of the line before it lands on the water, with the intention of keeping the line upstream of the fly and in the fishing lane.

To execute a reach cast, complete the basic back-and-forward cast. After the line straightens in the air in front of you, move the rod tip in the direction upstream of your casting target. Drop the fly line to the water. The fly will drift downstream to its target with a drag-free float. Finish the cast by pointing the rod tip back at your fly.

As with an on-the-water mend, additional line should be added to the cast, so that the fly reaches your target. If the line is held tight in the line hand in a fixed length, the reach move will drop the fly in a lane of water closer to the angler than intended. To counter this, the angler shoots line on the cast. Measure the distance needed to reach the target fish by false casting over it, and then shoot line on the final cast so that the fly goes beyond the target in the air. The reach will use up this additional line. Or, you can let line slide from your line hand through the guides while executing the reach,

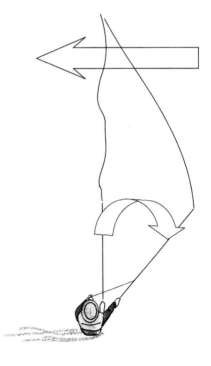

After the line straightens in the air on the final cast, move the rod in a direction upstream of your target. Drop the line to the water.

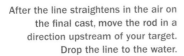

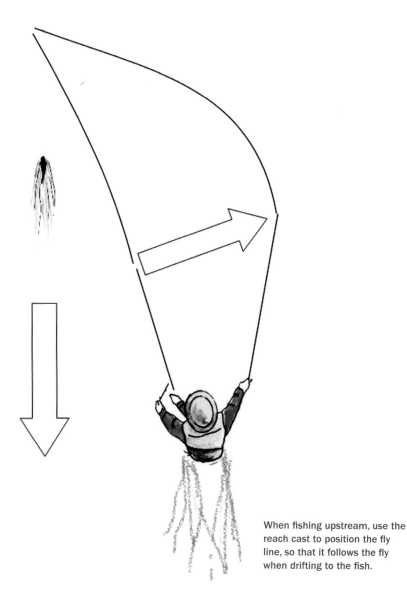

When fishing upstream, use the reach cast to position the fly line, so that it follows the fly when drifting to the fish.

pointing your rod tip upstream of the target. This last technique, referred to as a reach cast with a slide, or sliding reach cast, gives the angler more control over the cast.

Very effective when an angler is casting downstream, the reach cast is also a great technique for presenting the fly to a fish upstream of the angler. By positioning the fly line in the water to the side of the fly, the reach allows the fly to drift towards the fish without the line running over its head first.

S-Cast

If you are casting to a target that is directly downstream of your position, present with an S-cast. An S-cast will put curves in your line when it falls to the water.

To start, false cast over the target to determine the minimum length of line you need for the fly to drift down to the target. Shoot a few more feet of line to lengthen the cast enough so that your fly is beyond the target. On the final forward cast, after the fly line has straightened in the air, wave the rod tip back and forth. Once the fly line has dropped onto the water, you will find that the waving has created a series of S-curves in the line.

The S-curves create slack that will allow the fly to drift naturally for a longer period of time than a presentation without added line.

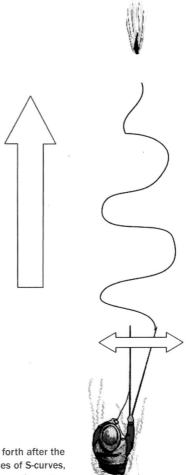

Wave the rod tip back and forth after the final cast to create a series of S-curves, adding slack to the line on the water.

When fishing downstream, wave the rod tip back and forth on the forward cast to create a series of S-curves. The curves add slack to the line on the water, so the current does not drag the fly.

The strength used to wave the rod tip will affect the amount of line cast into the S-curves. A vigorous wiggle will create S-curves that take up several feet of line, whereas a gentle wave will result in curves measured in inches.

The size of the curves depends on the strength used to wave the rod. A vigorous wave produces larger curves.

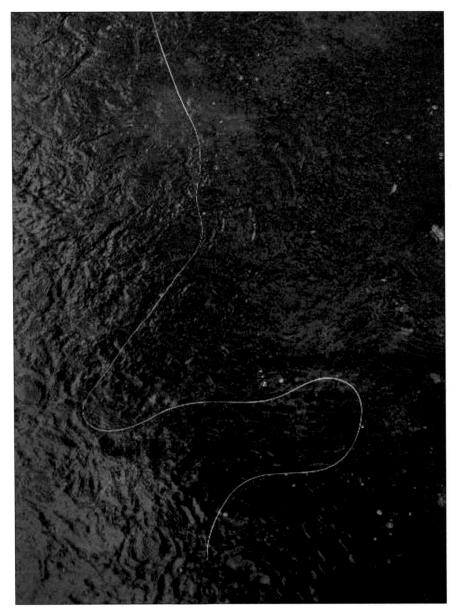

GUIDE TIP

If you are fishing in slow or clear water, false cast above a spot next to your intended target area without casting your line over the fish. By casting first to a practice target, you will be able to determine the length of line needed for the fly to drift over the fish, without spooking it with false casts over its head. When making the final cast, compensate for the difference between the distance from you to the target and you to the practice target.

Shock Cast or Bump Cast

One of the most basic casts used to add slack is the shock or bump cast. Simply put, after the line has straightened in the final forward cast, begin a partial back cast by accelerating the rod tip back several inches to a foot or two, and then drop the line to the surface. The resulting squiggle in the leader will allow the fly to float longer before it begins to drag.

Downstream Bump Cast

A casting option that will produce results similar to the S-cast is the downstream bump cast. This cast positions slack in the same current as your target fish and, ultimately, your fly. Preparation for the downstream bump cast is the same as for the S-cast: Measure the distance between you and the fish with a few false casts in the air above or near the target. Shoot additional line to extend your cast six to nine feet beyond the target. Cast your final forward cast. When the line has straightened in front of you in the air, bring your rod tip back toward you as if to begin another back cast. Do not complete the backcast; instead drop your line to the water.

The end result of this cast will be a fairly straight line of slack situated in the water parallel to the line leading to your fly.

Ultimately your slack is traveling at the same speed as your fly.

This cast is simple in concept, but difficult to execute without overdoing it. It requires control of the backcast movement just prior to laying the line on the water. The partial backcast movement may be slight, a light twitch

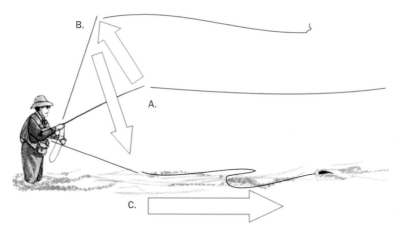

A. When the line has straightened in the air on the forward cast, bring your rod tip back as if to begin another cast.
B. Do not complete the back cast, instead drop your line to the water.
C. This cast ends with a fairly straight line of slack on the water parallel to the line leading to your fly.

The downstream bump cast puts slack line in the same current as the fly.

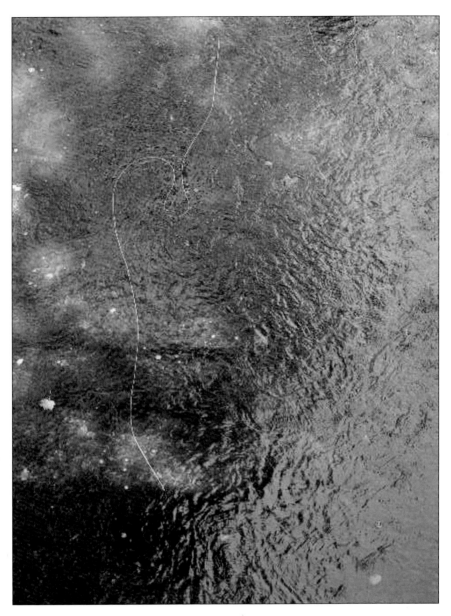

The line straightens as the slack drifts down the current without pulling on the fly.

upstream of the rod tip. Or it may be more extreme, with the rod tip moving several feet in the upstream direction. The results of the first version of the cast will be a few inches of slack line on the water, whereas the end result of the second version will be several feet of slack line.

GUIDE TIP

The ideal way to fish the far side of a current is to keep your line out of the fast water. This can be accomplished by standing in the current or holding the rod over the lane of faster water. If the lane of water is wider than the length of your rod, use a high-sticking method.

Keep your rod tip up instead of holding it low to the water. Point your rod tip in the direction of the fly, and follow it downstream while you continue to mend your line. Slide your line hand closer to the bottom guide to improve its position for setting the hook when a fish strikes.

Keep your line out of a fast current by holding your rod tip high in the air.
Photo Credit: Bert Darrow

CONTROLLING SLACK

Presentation is about your line, leader, and tippet. Mending and the casts described above control slack in your line and leader. What about when the tippet lands in a pile around your fly? This sloppy presentation usually turns away a fish. To avoid dropping the leader to the water in a heap, use a single haul on your forward cast. Just as the rod starts to accelerate forward on your cast, pull the line down a few inches with your line hand. The combination of the line at the top of your rod unfurling in front of you and the line toward the bottom of your rod being tugged back will increase the speed of the line as it opens up, causing the tippet to straighten. This leaves the fly clear of a nest of tippet and free to drift downstream without drag.

Controlling slack is important for both the nymph fisher and the dry fly angler. Drag can be a problem underwater as well as on the surface. Just think of the wake of a submarine instead of a motorboat, and you will understand. Presentation and drift are important throughout the water column, the vertical shaft from the riverbed to the water's surface.

A single haul in your final cast will increase line speed and straighten the tippet.

CASTING TARGET

An everyday mistake that is often overlooked is the repeated failure to hit the casting target. I've seen anglers go for a rising fish with casts that are consistently too long or too short and blame disinterest of the fish or poor fly selection for not getting a hit. It is frustrating for the angler who does not recognize the fault and consequently does not correct it. Missing the target area and not realizing it can be caused by a depth of vision problem or the low visibility of the fly.

Impaired Perspective

The height of an angler's eyes above the surface of the water affects his depth of vision. An angler wading deep in the water does not have the same perspective as an angler standing in a foot of water with his eyes five feet above the surface. The taller an angler or the higher his eyes above the water, the better his perspective and, assuming that casting techniques are equal, the easier it is to gauge distance and hit the target area.

To compensate for a height challenge, the angler should look for higher ground or stand on a submerged rock. If this is not feasible, the angler can cover the target area with different length casts. Always starting with a shorter cast so as not to run the line over the fish's head, the angler should drift the fly down a feeding lane several times to pass over where he thinks the fish is rising. If the fish does not rise to the fly, the next cast should be a few inches longer. A couple of casts later, a few more inches should be added to the cast. This trial-and-error method can be continued until the angler is sure that the fly is drifting on the far side of the fish, having covered the entire area near where the fish is rising.

A less methodical approach is for the angler to gauge the position of his fly in comparison to a natural insect taken by the rising fish and shorten or lengthen his next cast accordingly. This may be accomplished by noting the location of the fly in comparison to insects on the water when the fly lands and by watching the fleet of naturals and sole imitation drift toward the fish. This may take several attempts as the angler hones in on a natural.

Visibility of Fly

There are many times when a dry fly is not conspicuous enough for the angler to see it. Low light, a dark fly on dark water, a small or sparsely hackled offering all affect the visibility of a fly. If the angler can't see his fly, he will probably miss the fish rising to it. In this situation, a visual aid or strike indicator can be attached to the line. A dry-fly fisher's visual aids would be a lighter-colored fly or a gob of fluorescent floatant putty. The indicator should be attached at least a foot above the fly and preferably two feet so as not to spook fish. If a fish rises while the indicator is drifting near, the angler should set the hook.

An angler wading deep will find it challenging to gauge casting distance.

CHAPTER 10

PRESENTING THE FLY

The hatch chart at the fly shop said Hoppers. I saw the list of flies written in thick chalk letters. When I got to the water, I tied a Size 8 Stimulator onto my client's line. He plopped the fly on the stream near the bank and let it drift with the current, a dead drift with no action as if it were a terrestrial insect caught in the layer of film on the water. Nothing happened. At the end of the drift, he lifted the fly and cast again. He repeated this action a few times. We were disappointed, and I was perplexed. Periodically, fish rose next to the bank, but they were not taking anything resembling a grasshopper. Suddenly, I saw it . . . "Give the fly some action on the next drift," I said. "Bump it around, throw extra slack in the line, anything to make the fly hop a bit." With the next cast and a live action drift, a fish came zooming up from the depths and closed its mouth over the bushy Stimulator. After the fish had been played and released, the angler looked at me with a question in his eyes. "Stoneflies," I said. "There are Golden Stones laying eggs on the water."

The Stimulator is a versatile fly that can be used to imitate several different insects. With a dead drift, the Stimulator floats with the typical stillness of a grasshopper blown onto the water. But, when the drift is altered by the introduction of action, the fly becomes an ovipositing Stonefly striking the surface of the water to release its eggs. The fish were keyed onto this insect and its behavioral characteristics.

A COMMON MISTAKE

The prevailing thought seems to be that dry flies, especially mayfly duns, should be presented with a dead drift, which delivers no action to the lure at all. Anglers acknowledge that caddis hop or skitter on the water before taking off. Even so, most of the anglers I watch habitually use a dead drift for anything they float on the surface.

Despite this, March Brown, Gray Fox, and Green Drake duns are tied to represent mayflies that move on the water instead of floating immobile before springing into flight. Egg-laying females of many insect species hit the water to dislodge their eggs, and some even dive under the surface.

I've only mentioned dry flies here, but nymphs and emergers are also divided into categories of action.

Many fly fishers use the same technique to fish most of their flies: drifting dries, nymphs, and even streamers at the speed of the current and occasionally remembering to tug on the line a little for some added action. But, each natural insect comes with its own behavioral traits, which make an imprint on the fish. If the imitation does not act like the real thing, the fish will not look at it.

THE FIX

Match the action of your fly to the action of the natural it is imitating.

An important step in the preparation for a day of fishing is determining which insects will be active on the water. Find out not just the name of the natural, but its typical characteristics as well.

Match the action of your fly to the action of the natural for a complete imitation that will entice a fish.

For example, when fishing in March Brown season, be prepared to cast your lure into the riffles and swim it with a technique that alternates between raising and lowering the nymph to imitate the swimming movement of the natural, then drifting the fly motionlessly to mimic the frozen body of the natural caught in the current.

Even if you did not refresh your knowledge of insects and their movements before getting on the water, take a first-hand lesson from the naturals that are active while you are fishing. You won't be able to see the subsurface activity of the nymphs, but you can observe the insects on top of the water. If they are jumping or actively moving on the surface, give your dry fly action to match.

ACTION OF THE FLY

To mimic a natural insect, be aware of the kind of movement you can impart to your imitation fly when manipulating it in the water. Familiarize yourself with the action by dropping the fly to the water near you, but make sure it is tied to your leader first. Move the fly, retrieve it, watch it drift. Study the motion of your lure for a few minutes.

Once you know what your imitation can do, play with it so as to simulate the action of the natural insect you are trying to match. See what happens when you twitch the rod or strip in line.

GUIDE TIP

The first question to answer before presenting any fly is: dead drift or live action? You are trying to imitate what the natural insect does. Does the insect drift with the current, necessitating a dead drift presentation of your fly? Or does the insect move, requiring live action in the manipulation of your imitation?

NYMPHS

Nymphs can be sorted into a few categories with similar characteristics. Learn the traits of each category, determine which category matches the active insect, and you will know how to fish your fly.

Casemaker/Netspinner Larvae

- Certain netspinner larvae move downstream from stone to stone by means of a rappelling white or light brown silk.
- To imitate the silk, whiten the first six inches of the tippet above the fly. I use a White-Out pen. Attach split-shot a few inches above the whitened tippet.
- When drifting the fly, move your rod tip gently up and down to hop the weight downstream. The nymph will appear to move from rock to rock by using its fine silk as a rappelling rope.

Clingers

- Just before emerging, clingers migrate from the faster current to slower water, where they swim actively.
- Work your fly to the front and sides of rocks where fish might be holding.
- Concentrate your fishing in pocket water and just below the riffles.

Crawlers

- As the water warms, crawler larvae move about actively. They climb to the top of subsurface rocks, where they are more exposed to the current and to trout.
- When adrift in faster water, the insects remain rigid and should be dead-drifted.
- In slower currents, the naturals swim awkwardly. Introduce action through a retrieve or rod movement to animate the fly.

Swimmers

- Swimmers are active insects that move quickly.

GUIDE TIP

To add action to a nymph on a windy day, tie on a fluffy strike indicator. Grease it with floatant. Do anything to give it a high profile. The strike indicator will bob on the surface waves and when the breeze blows. The nymph will in turn bob up and down under the water's surface.

- Try various techniques for adding movement when you drift these nymphs.
- At the end of the drift, swing the fly toward the stream bank. Allow time for fish to follow and take the fly before pulling it out of water.

EMERGERS

There are two basic categories defining the behavior of natural insects emerging from the water to their adult stage:

If the insect emerges from the bottom, it springs from the riverbed to the surface. When it reaches the surface, it may drift while shedding its pupal skin or immediately run or hop across the water to launch into the air to reach a rock.

If the insect rests at the water's surface before transforming to its adult stage, it is a surface emerger.

DRY FLIES

Adult insects are imitated with dry flies drifted on top of the water with action that matches their behavioral characteristics.

If the natural insect drifts motionlessly on the water's surface as the wings dry in preparation for flying away, float your fly on the current with a dead drift free of drag.

If the natural moves across the water propelled by its own energy, perhaps fluttering its drying wings or hopping on the surface in preparation for taking off, present your imitation with live action.

Techniques for giving live action to a fly are limited only by the conditions of the environment and the features of the fishing gear.

Skating a Fly

The best place to skate a fly is in the tail of a pool, where the water is fast but smooth.

A simple method for skating a fly is the two steps forward/one step back presentation:

- Grease the fly and the tippet with floatant.
- Cast the line across or downstream.
- Raise the rod tip in the air to move or skitter the fly a few inches at most.
- Lower the rod tip while retrieving slack.

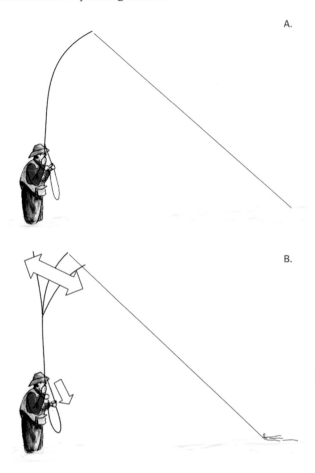

A. To present with a high stick and wiggle, raise rod tip in the air to about eleven o'clock.
B. Strip in line while wiggling the rod tip.

- Repeat the last two steps until the fly is close to you.
- Start again.

Another way to add skating action to a dry fly is the high stick and wiggle presentation.

- Choose a fly with a thick hackle that will hold the body of the imitation just above the water surface.
- Make sure that your tippet is one size heavier than usual, as takes from fish can be explosive with this presentation method.
- Grease the tippet with floatant or line dressing.
- Cast across and downstream with a straight-line cast.

- As soon as the fly hits the water, raise your rod arm in the air until your rod tip points to about eleven o'clock.
- Strip in line while wiggling the line with your rod tip.
- The fly will skip across the surface.
- After you skate the fly for three or four feet, drop the tip of the rod and follow the line downstream.

This technique is very effective for attracting fish taking active insects. The drag-free float gives the fish a chance to inspect the prey, and another wiggle usually drives it to the surface.

Skating a fly does not work well on riffled water because the broken surface pulls the fly under. It also does not work well in slow water where fish are easily spooked and have more time to inspect the fly.

Presenting with a Plop

If you are imitating an ovipositing caddis or stonefly, drop your fly heavily onto the water to match the natural insect's behavior as it lays eggs. Twitch the fly and let it rest, then twitch again. If you are fishing with terrestrials, present with a plop, but twitch less frequently. Terrestrials get caught in the film layer on the surface of the water and, if small or light, have a difficult time moving.

WET FLIES

Wet flies can also be fished with either a dead drift or simulated action. If you are not sure of the behavioral characteristics of the naturals that are active in the water while you are fishing, try both methods. Cast across the current and slightly downstream of where you are standing. Let the fly drift with a dead swing, no action. After casting a few times to the same water with a set length of line, cast to the same spot again. This time, however, add movement to your fly as you retrieve: Strip in a few inches of line, stop, strip in a few inches of line, stop. Try three or four casts and action drifts across the identical path. Then lengthen your line by a foot, and repeat these steps. Continue until you have covered the area.

STREAMERS

Streamers are tied to mimic smaller fish, leeches, and other creatures swimming in the water. They can be fished with a dead drift or live-action presentation.

To dead drift a streamer, cast the fly across the water and slightly downstream from where you are standing. Let the fly swing in the current without adjusting the line or the fly: no mend, no tug, no retrieve.

After a few casts with a dead-drift swing, cast the fly to the same water, and retrieve it with a lifelike motion. Secure the line under the index finger of your rod hand. Reach with your line hand to hold the line leading from under your index finger to the reel. Strip a few inches of fly line from the water by tugging with your line hand. Drop the line that you retrieved to the water between your reel and where the line is secured by your rod hand index finger. Stop and let the fly drift a little. Strip in a few inches of line again. Repeat this technique until most of the line has been retrieved.

Draw the attention of larger fish by creating your own food chain: a small baitfish being chased by another. To achieve this effect, attach a weighted streamer to the end of your leader. Add an unweighted streamer as a second fly by tying it to the bend of the hook of the first fly. Cast the two flies. Let them sink for several seconds before beginning your retrieve. Use an animated tug to retrieve the flies.

GUIDE TIP

To cast streamers or heavily weighted flies a distance, do not false cast, as the heavy fly may pull the line down and cause the hook to catch on it and tangle. To avoid creating a bird's nest, pick the line up off the water in your back cast and drop the line back to the water after the forward cast. Without giving the fly time to sink, make another back cast. Shoot line to lengthen the cast, and let the line drop to the water again on the forward cast. Continue this casting until the line reaches the desired length. Then, fish your fly.

It is wise to start your fishing by aiming at targets closer to your position and casting to distant targets afterwards, so the fly line does not disturb the water you plan to fish later.

CHAPTER 11

HOOK, PLAY, NET

"The fish in this river must be a different breed," a client/angler said to me one day. "Why is that?" I asked. "I can't catch them. They will go for my fly, but I can't bring them to the net. They always get away or break off," she answered (and this is a woman who has fished for many years). "My husband won't even come to this river," she added. I was amazed. Her husband is a more accomplished angler than the woman who was confessing her frustration.

I have often been asked about the reactions of the fish on this or that stream and been told by anglers that they cannot hook fish on certain rivers where the fish respond differently from those on someone's home water.

Anglers leaving their home waters to fish in different surroundings or for a different species often forget to adjust their techniques to match the new environment. A redfish fisherman in the middle of a trout stream has to set a hook with less force to avoid ripping it out of the trout's softer jaw. A trout fisher trying for spawning salmon needs a little more patience while the salmon typically ignores the fly until it is completely annoyed. The angler who regularly fishes in fast currents must land his fly lightly on the water with pinpoint precision when visiting a slow-moving pool.

A COMMON MISTAKE

Novice fly fishers wait to feel a tug on the line before reacting to a hit by a fish. Experienced anglers may be so distracted by fishing methods that they are not ready for the unexpected take. Anglers of all skill levels who are simply relaxed and enjoying the day may fail to notice the subtle bump of a fly being swallowed by a fish. Whatever the reason, anglers often miss the opportunity to set the hook and, as a result, lose out on a fishing moment. This lapse can happen frequently enough that it becomes part of the day's tally: "I caught five and missed eight."

THE FIX

The first lesson for every angler on the topic of setting the hook is to remember that fish will take a fly at any time. Fish don't read books or follow a sequence of instructions. They grab what looks edible before it floats by. Therefore, the angler should be prepared to set a hook as soon as the fly nears the water.

The second lesson is a reminder about the "Stop, Look, and Listen" suggestion made in Chapter 5. While observing what is happening on the water, make note of the behavior of any fish feeding at the surface. Your reaction pace must match the speed of the fish.

SETTING THE HOOK

The essential note about setting the hook is that it should pierce the jaw of the fish and stay in place while you reel it in.

A well-hooked 'bow ready for release.

Beyond this theory, there is no common standard. Variable fishing conditions influence technique.

Rod Action

Take into account the stiffness of the rod. The stiff nature of a fast-action rod makes it a great tool for distance casting. This feature also requires a gentle touch when setting the hook, especially with a lighter leader or tippet.

Conversely, a slow-action rod may be too flexible to secure a hook. If you continue to lose fish with a slow-action rod, set the hook by moving the rod tip in one direction and pulling line with your line hand in the opposite direction.

Water Features

It is rare that an angler controls setting a hook in fast-moving water. Generally, the fish hooks itself in fast water or spits the fly out before you have time to react. To improve fast-water techniques when fishing with a nymph, set the hook every time the strike indicator or the fly line hesitates, moves upstream, or dips into the water. In other words, you should react to everything.

Slow water requires different techniques. In slow-moving currents or pools, fish have time to look at each possible bite of food as it drifts by. Setting a hook is not difficult, but having the patience to wait until the hook is in the fish's mouth is. If the water is clear, you may be able to watch a fish take your subsurface fly. Don't move the line until the fish has closed its mouth over the hook. If you can't see fish, use a strike indicator or watch the fly line for twitches.

Length of Line on the Water

If you are casting to targets at a distance from your position and have a lot of line on the water when a fish takes your fly, you will have to do more to set the hook than pinch the line or move the rod tip a couple of feet.

The most common movement used to set a hook is raising the rod tip high in the air above the angler's head in an effort to lift the line off the water. A more effective method to set the hook takes advantage of the friction created by water adhering to the fly line floating on the surface. When a fish takes your fly, keep the rod parallel to the water, and move the tip away from the line on the water. Whether you have been casting a long line or a shorter one, the resistance will help set the hook.

Anglers who aim at targets sixty or more feet away often find their reaction time is too slow to set the hook with so much line on the water. They will improve their catch numbers by using this technique. Anglers who fish with

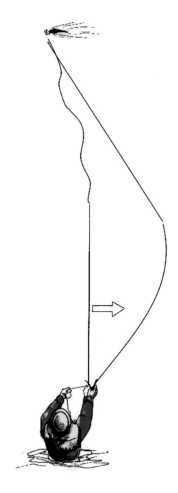

Set the hook by moving the rod tip in the direction away from the line floating on the water while keeping the rod parallel to the surface.

shorter lines will also improve their percentages with this technique. Everyone wins, except the fish.

Breaking off Fish

Anyone who has broken off a fish, and that would be every one of us, may wish to review this list of solutions to avoid such heartbreaking loss.

Are your fish breaking off upon impact? Or are they breaking off while you are playing them?

UPON IMPACT

If you lose the fish and your fly remains on the line, you may be reacting to the take too quickly.

Concentrate on the initial resistance of the fish when you set the hook. If you are reacting too quickly, you may not feel any resistance other than the friction of the water, or you may sense a ripping as you tear the fly out of the fish before the hook is set. If you are fishing with a dry fly, you may even be able to see that you are pulling the fly away before the fish has even closed its mouth. To paraphrase the words of the great Simon and Garfunkel: *Slow down. You move too fast. You've got to make the moment last.* Let the fish take the fly before you try to take it back.

If you lose the fish and your fly breaks off, you may be using too much force in your reaction to the hit.

Don't haul back hard on the rod to set the hook. Move the rod tip slightly (even just one to two feet) in the direction away from the fish while tightening your

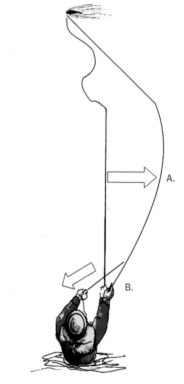

If there is slack in your line when a fish takes, set the hook by moving the rod in one direction (A) and pulling the line in the opposite direction with your line hand (B).

hold on the line with your line hand. If you need to take up slack while setting the hook, swing the rod tip in one direction in a movement that is parallel to the water's surface while pulling the line in the other direction with your line hand.

If you lose the fish and your fly, you may be experiencing a breakdown of your equipment.

Is the Knot Holding?

Check the end of your tippet where the fly had been. Has your tippet formed a curl at the end like a pig's tail or a corkscrew? As mentioned in Chapter 4, a curl indicates that your knot has slipped. Review the steps in the knot you used to tie a fly onto the tippet. If you are tying a clinch knot with a fine tippet size 6x, 7x, 8x, and smaller), use the improved clinch knot. If you are fishing a large fly, thread the tippet through the eye of the hook twice before continuing to tie the knot. Remember to wet the tippet before tightening the knot, so that you are not burning the tippet, thereby stressing and weakening it before you begin to fish. You will know that the line has been compromised if it becomes wavy. When you seat the knot, pull the standing leader or tippet, the side that runs up the rod to the reel, while holding the fly tight. Do not pull the tag (the loose end of the tippet) or the fly to tighten the knot.

Is Your Tippet Old?

Tippet material has a shelf life and ages even faster when exposed to the sun or to extreme weather conditions. Nowadays, many manufacturers provide an expiration date on leader and tippet packaging. If you don't see a date, but purchased your tippet more than three years ago, buy a new spool. You don't want to continue to lose fish because your equipment has worn out.

WHILE PLAYING THE FISH

If you lose the fish and your fly remains on the line, you may have relaxed the pressure on the line.

Make sure that there is always a bend in the rod once you have hooked a fish.

When the fish swims away from you, let it take line, but maintain some pressure just by holding the rod in a bent position. When the fish stops

To play a fish successfully, maintain a bend in the rod, and eliminate slack from the line.

swimming away or turns and swims toward you, reel line in to keep it taut. If it swims toward you faster than you can reel, move the rod tip away from the fish to maintain a bend while you reel or strip in.

If you are playing the fish on the reel and your tippet breaks, ease the drag before your next cast by turning the knob on your reel. Read Chapter 4, "Line, Leader, and Tippet," about adjusting the drag on your reel. If your reel is not adjustable or the drag is on the lightest setting, you can avoid losing a fish by playing it better. Give in to the fish more, especially if you have a stiff rod. When the fish pulls the line or swims away, move your casting arm in its direction. Be flexible: Use your arm as a spring, softening the pull of the fish on the line. Fishing equipment is made to give: The tippet, the leader and even the line will stretch; the rod will bend. Let your body do the same by moving with the fish so as to cushion the shock.

If you strip in line and drop it at your feet instead of winding it onto the reel, you are playing the fish with your hands, not off the reel. Remember to release the line in your hand when the fish darts away. You don't want to be caught with your hand holding the line so tight that the leader is stressed and breaks when the fish runs. Do, however, keep some pressure on the line as it runs out, so that the fish eventually tires and stops fighting.

Is Your Gear the Correct Size or Weight?

Pay attention to what is happening in the environment around you. If you are fishing a streamer in the fall for spawning brown trout, remember that these fish are very aggressive and will hit a fly hard—as will rainbows feeding in fast water, or brookies chasing emerging caddis. If your gear is too light for aggressive fishing, you may have to switch to a different rod, leader, or tippet. Match your equipment and your technique to the fishing of the moment.

A fish breaking off usually means there is too much tension: in old tippet that doesn't stretch easily, in stiff rods that are not pliable enough to play fish on light tackle, in lines that are secured too tightly against the pull of the prey, and most importantly, in an angler's muscles that aren't relaxed enough to serve as a cushion. So, when you are on the water, run through this checklist, paying particular attention to the relaxing of muscle tension. You may still break off some fish, but you will enjoy playing many more.

PLAYING THE FISH

Rod Work

As mentioned before, a key element in playing the fish is keeping a bend in the rod. If the fish becomes airborne, however, the rule changes. When a fish jumps, lower the rod tip until the fish enters the water again. The weight of a fish is often enough to break the tippet. Lowering the rod releases tension in the line, so that a fish will not break the tippet or the leader if it lands on it. This precaution is often referred to as bowing to the fish: When a fish jumps, bow to it with your rod.

Steering Fish

Fish swim away from anything that spooks them and will use the familiar as shelter. In deep pools, depth is shelter, so a fish might dive deep. In water with overhanging banks, a hooked fish may swim under the overhang. If there are boulders or submerged logs or branches, a hooked fish may seek refuge around these obstacles. And a fish may just swim upstream or downstream, putting distance between itself and danger.

A universal truth is that a hooked fish will race away from what is tugging it. If a fish is hooked on the right side of its jaw, chances are that fish will swim to the left. If the fish is hooked on the left side of its jaw, it will probably swim to the right and away from whatever is pulling at it from that side.

Take advantage of these basic instincts to play your fish. Put pressure on the fish with your line to direct it to swim where you want it to swim. If the fish is swimming across the water to your left, maneuver the line, so that it feels pull from the left and will veer to the right. And if the fish runs to the right, move the line so that the tug is from the right, causing the fish to run in the opposite direction.

Controlling Fish

A startled fish will fight or run harder. If a fish is not stressed, it will not fight.

A fish being pulled straight up to the water's surface will fight hard against this unnatural force. If the angle of the line is not as severe, the fish will not fight as fiercely.

Hold the rod parallel and low to the water to ease the fight of the fish.

Test this theory yourself by playing a hooked fish with the rod parallel to the water and the rod tip close to the surface of the water. Compare the fight to when a fish is played with the rod tip up high.

GUIDE TIP

If you are fishing with a long leader and cannot reach the fish to net it, do not hesitate to reel your leader into the tiptop of your rod.

Don't catch yourself off-balance. Reel in the line to bring the fish close to your net, and don't worry about the leader running through the guides.

As long as you have a smooth connection from leader to line, you should not snag the guides. It is a good idea to tire the fish before bringing the line so far in, but if the fish does run again and draws the connecting loop or knot out of the guides again, you must simply pay attention and manipulate the line and rod to avoid any snagging.

NETTING THE FISH

How often does an angler hook and play a fish, then reel it in for the release, only to have the fish bolt at the sight of the net? When the fish slips off the hook in a clean break, the release is complete, but a bit disappointing for the angler who cherishes a moment up close with his prey. Too many times, however, the fish snaps the tippet and leaves the scene with a hook in its jaw and filament trailing alongside. This happens most frequently when the fish moves suddenly to escape. The effort can catch the fly fisher unprepared, with rod, line, leader, and hands not in position to cushion the run. A sharp move often stresses the leader and causes it to break.

I admit that I have plucked some interesting flies from the mouths of previously caught fish, but it is always with a sigh. Even if the hook falls out naturally in time in accordance with popular theory, an angler never wants to impair a fish unnecessarily.

Instead of thrashing the net in the water in an attempt to land the fish, try a calmer method. It will not be as amusing to the fly fishers around you—who, believe me, are sympathizing with you even as they chuckle—but it will be less frustrating for you and easier on both the angler and the fish. Before

Guide the fish
to the net.

reeling the fish in close, dip your net in the water and hold it under the surface. Guide the fish to the net.

GUIDE TIP

When playing a fish in order to net it, work the fish to a position upstream of where you are standing. When the fish is directly upstream of you, drop the rod tip to the water to release all pressure. Without a line tugging at its jaw, the fish will instantly calm and settle on the bottom of the stream. Slowly dip the net underwater directly downstream of the fish. Raise the tip of your rod. The fish will turn downstream to swim away from the line and directly into the net.

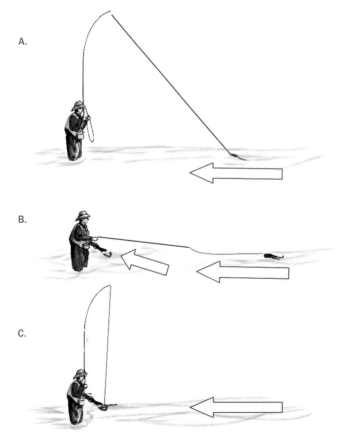

A.

B.

C.

A. When playing a hooked fish, steer it to upstream of your position.
B. Drop the rod tip to the water to release all pressure and dip the net underwater downstream of the fish.
C. Raise the tip of your rod and net the fish when it turns to swim down-stream.

RELEASING FISH

Fly fishers in general should be applauded for their catch-and-release practices. Even though some anglers do keep fish, most release them back into the
water. The goal is to let the fish live and perhaps to be caught again some day,
but even the best intentions can't save a fish that has been handled incorrectly.

It pains me to see anglers injure fish, especially when they are trying to
revive it and set it free. The damage is not always immediately evident, so the
angler remains unaware of the harm he has caused and thus has no reason to
correct his method of releasing a fish.

When planning to release a fish, play the fish to tire it enough to bring
it in, but not to the point at which it is stressed or exhausted beyond reviving.

Handling Fish

The less you touch a fish, the healthier it will remain after being released.
Ideally, a fish is reeled in close to an angler standing in the water or leaning
over the side of a boat. The angler reaches down and uses his hemostats to

To cradle a fish, hold your hands loosely around its body while it floats in the water.

remove the hook from the fish's mouth. Then, he cradles his hands around the fish as it floats in the water, facing into the current.

The idea is to protect the fish until it is able to revive and swim away. This situation depends on a number of factors: the hook set lightly in the jaw of the fish, the angler positioned securely, the fish waiting patiently for the hook extraction.

In the real world, most anglers touch a fish with their hands or a net. In these situations, there are a few points to remember that will promote the release of a fish in the healthiest manner possible.

To touch a fish, use bare, wet hands, which are less abrasive than dry or gloved fingers.

Use wet hands when touching fish to preserve their protective coating.

Keep away from the sensitive areas of a fish: gills and the lateral line. Photo credit: Bert Darrow

This preserves the layer of slime covering a fish. The slime coating protects fish from bacteria, parasites, and disease. When it is rubbed away, the fish will be susceptible to everything and can die before regenerating the coating.

Catch-and-release nets are available with bags made of rubberized or treated mesh, designed to do little damage to the fish. Even so, wet the net before bringing a fish into it. Anything dry will scrape away some of the slime coating.

When handling a fish, do not squeeze it or touch sensitive areas such as the gills or the lateral line.

Gills work like a bellows, opening and closing to push water through. Oxygen in the water is absorbed into the gills, allowing a fish to breathe just as lungs work for a human. If a fish is held around its gills, it cannot work them and will suffocate. The lateral line is a sensory organ that runs along each side of the fish. It allows a fish to feel sound waves and motion. Maintaining a tight hold on the lateral line is akin to boxing the ears of a fish.

Removing the Hook

To remove the hook from a fish, plant yourself in a stable position with secure footholds.

Balance yourself with solid footing before removing the hook.

Remove the hook from a fish floating in the confines of a net.

The fish should be kept under the surface of the water, held firmly, but not squeezed with one hand or by floating in the confines of the bag of the net.

Fly fishing forceps and pliers are tools of choice for removing a hook from the lips of most fish. Grasp the shank of the hook with the tool, and back the hook out of the lip.

Barbless hooks should slide right out. A hook with a barb may take a little more manipulating. Remember this and crimp the barbs of your hooks before you fish next time.

While removing the hook, make sure the fish remains completely in the water.

Reviving a Fish

Work underwater as much as possible, keeping fish, net, and hands submerged. To revive a fish, face it upstream, so that the water flows into its mouth and through its gills from front to back.

Use forceps to back a hook out of the puncture.

If the current is heavy, move to quieter water, or shield the fish with your legs. The flow of water will help revive the fish, but a fast current can stress it further.

The old method of reviving a fish by rocking it back and forth in the current has been successfully challenged. The rocking forces water to flow

To revive a fish, face it upstream, protected from the force of the current. The fish will swim away when it has recovered.

through the gills in the wrong direction, damaging the fish. Just cradle the fish gently in the water, and let the animal recover on its own. This interaction between angler and fish can be the most satisfying part of the fishing experience.

Taking Pictures

Even the most environmentally conscious angler wants to take home a photo of his amazing catch. If the fish is revived properly, there is no reason not to snap a shot or two.

Leave the fish in the water until you are ready to take the picture. Make sure the camera is on and focused. If you have a fishing buddy nearby, ask him to take the photo. This is much easier than trying to do it all yourself!

If you are raising the fish into the air, hold it in a horizontal position parallel to the water with two hands under its belly. Do not hang the fish vertically, a position that will disturb the inner organs and can kill the fish. Remember not to squeeze the lateral lines or the gills.

Take a good picture that shows off both you and the fish.

Pay attention to how you are holding the fish. Position your hands and arms on the side away from the camera, so they are not covering the fish in the photo.

The fish is well supported, and the angler's face is clear of glasses. This is a good photo of a fly fisherman and his beautiful brown trout. Photo credit: Al Caucci

The fish is impressive, but we can't recognize the angler. Push up the brim of your hat!
Photo credit: Shannon Brightman

Push up your hat brim, if possible, so that your face is not shaded.

Remove your glasses, if they are attached by a string, and let them hang around your neck.

Secure your fly rod under your arm, or hand it off to someone else.

Smile. Then, release the fish gently back into the water.

CHAPTER 12

SAFETY ON THE WATER

A few years ago, fishermen on the Beaverkill in New York watched in horror when a man lost his footing as he tried to cross the river at a dangerous junction and drowned in the heavy spring current. The flows from two incoming rivers create a turbulence in that spot that is impossible to wade through in the calmest season and fatal to attempt in high water. The hapless young man was fishing with friends who had waded across the river farther upstream. Without first hiking upstream, he picked his way across the water until the river swept him away.

A COMMON MISTAKE

While concentrating on the many details of fishing, such as the drift of a fly or the rise of a fish, anglers often ignore some of the dangers. They wade a little too deep to be one step closer to a fish that's just out of the reach of their casts. A bob or two or a misstep and the angler finds water pouring down his waders.

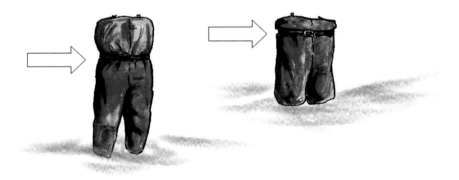

Wear your wading belt at your waist in shallow water. Raise it high in deep water.

Fishing in wet waders is uncomfortable and can quickly chill an angler—both ways to mar a day of fishing.

THE FIX

Don't just wear your wading belt. Use it. When you are wading in shallow water, keep the belt at your waist. When you move to deeper water, move the belt up your body, so that it circles your chest. If you step in too deep and water spills over the top of your waders, the section that would become filled is only from your belted chest up.

GUIDE TIP

For the belt to be effective, it should be cinched securely and not hanging loosely around your hips.

FALLING IN

A dunk in the water is a potential hazard of river wading. Clumsy boots, rolling rocks, slippery stones, and a strong current are all factors that can lead to a fall.

Most slips occur close to shore where an angler relaxes and pays more attention to the bank than to the riverbed. A fall in shallow water bruises knees and egos, but is easy to recover from.

It is the deep-water or heavy-current plunges that are most dangerous. Prepare for deep water by sliding your wading belt higher on your body and tightening it. Use your wading staff to probe for holes in the riverbed or unseen rocks.

If you slip in a heavy current and can't stand, turn so you float on your back with your feet pointing downstream. Bend your knees slightly. Use your legs as springs to push off any rocks you may encounter as you travel downriver. As you float downstream, breathe in at the top of a standing wave, and hold your breath when you dip into a trough.

Don't panic. In most situations, you will be pushed to shore when the current slows.

You should never wade in floodwaters or heavy rapids. But, if you find yourself in fast water, remember that churning water is full of oxygen. You won't float as easily. If you are caught in white water, it is easy to become disoriented and lose which direction is up and which is down. Drop your rod, and try to swim. Rough surface water may be full of air, but lower water is swimmable. Get down to the riverbed, and use your feet to push up to the surface. You will have more control of your float if you are able to move at a speed different from the current—whether slower or faster—so keep stroking.

If someone else falls in and is floating downstream, make sure you are safe before trying to rescue him. It is better to extend a branch or throw a rope to someone than to swim into rapids yourself.

Fishing has its dangers, but if you are familiar with emergency procedures, you will be better prepared in the face of an urgent situation.

FISHING ALONE

It seems to be part of a rite of passage for fly fishers. Many anglers have marked this rite, telling cherished tales about the times they have fished alone. Unfortunately, the act of fishing without a buddy does not register as a

A matter of safety, it's also much more fun to fish with someone who can take pictures of your memorable catch.

mistake with many anglers, although I notice that, whenever someone starts a story about fishing and adds that he was alone, there is always a pause, as if the storyteller were waiting to be reprimanded.

Anyone who spends time in the outdoors should know better. You should not fish alone. It's simply not safe. There are big reasons why: an incapacitating injury, getting lost, or a fatal accident. And there are smaller reasons, such as sustaining a minor injury or running into unfriendly strangers.

Fishing a river alone in the wilderness is foolhardy, but even a stream that runs through the woods behind your house holds potential for danger.

Admittedly, there is a delicious freedom in grabbing a fly rod and running off to the water for unfettered fishing, but being able to share the experience with someone else adds its own element of pleasure.

To prove this point, just think of the stories you have told of the near-misses you have had when fishing, or of the accidents themselves. What if there had been a serious accident, and no one was around?

Be smart, but don't cramp your fishing. Pick a buddy whose fishing preferences match your own. If you like to stay on the water for hours and hours, make sure your buddy has the same fortitude. If you enjoy moving

Many anglers have walked back and forth in search of an exit path hidden by foliage or brush.

from one spot to another, find an explorer. It may be as simple as arranging to meet up with an angler you see regularly when you fish your favorite spot. Your fishing buddy does not have to be your best friend, just someone who also needs a contact on the water.

And for those times when you carry your rod out the door to fish in the backyard, leave a note.

LOSING YOUR WAY ON THE WATER

This slip-up happens often enough that I keep a growing list of the places where fly fishers have missed their exit points from the water and had to scramble up banks farther downstream to get out. Those who admit to having lost their way do so with a chuckle, often rueful with the memory of scraped skin or, worse, ripped waders. One angler I know still has a scar on his cheek where a branch whipped his face as he struggled through dense brush.

Identify a distinct marker that will guide you to the exit path away from the water. Make note of it when you are standing in the water. Everything looks different when your feet are on the riverbed, two feet below the level of the ground. Confirm that your marker is visible each time you fish the spot. If you fished a pool in the early season and return to it a few weeks later, you will discover that landmarks may be obscured by new foliage. The tree scarred by lightning may be hidden by fresh growth of a neighboring tree, or it may have fallen down.

What seems a trivial point has been the cause of concern and stress for a number of anglers who have wandered up and down rivers trying to find their way home.

This is the wrong way to end a day of fishing.

GUIDE TIP

Carry a couple of strips of brightly colored material in your vest to tie onto branches to make your own landmarks. Remember to retrieve the strips when you leave the water.

Tie a bright ribbon onto a branch to mark your exit from the water.

FLY FISHING BY SEASON

The section on fishing each season illustrates practical applications of the tips and notes discussed in the first chapters. Stream conditions, weather, time of day, and season all contribute to changes in trout-feeding behavior. These elements will affect each decision you make in your approach and presentation to the fish.

Spring, pg. 127

Summer, pg. 137

Autumn, pg. 147

Winter, pg. 155

CHAPTER 13

SPRING FLY FISHING

A trio of anglers hired me to organize their outing, looking to take advantage of the many hatches that can appear in one day during the height of spring fishing. Good friends, the three anglers each brought different skill levels and fishing preferences to the water. Sandy, a flyfishing traditionalist with fishing experience in many parts of the country, seems to need a guide to hook most of his fish. Walter, a dry-fly purist, has unrivalled fishing abilities and experience. And good-natured Len will cast any fly that is working at a particular time.

Walter was easy. I tied on a succession of dries to match the hatches that appeared at different hours: Blue-Winged Olives, March Browns, the last of the Hendricksons and Red Quills, and finally March Brown spinners toward evening. He attracted fish every six or eight casts.

Len was given a mixture of flies throughout the day, using everything from nymphs and emergers to duns and finally spinners. He even swung streamers through the water. For every four fish caught by Walter, Len had a fish in his net. This was typical for these guys, and a good day for Len.

Sandy posed more of a challenge. He wanted to fish dries like Walter, but did not have the skill level to imitate the insects as well. I tied a March Brown nymph onto Sandy's tippet and prayed that his erratic presentation would match the swimming motion of the natural. His second cast brought in the first fish of the day, a big brown trout that impressed the group. Later, Sandy changed to an Isonychia nymph, another fly that requires an active presentation, and got more hook-ups. He also fished dry flies to round out his experience.

At the end of the day, when the three anglers compared notes, they were surprised to discover that their successes had come from differing lists of flies. This is the benefit of spring fly fishing at its peak.

A COMMON MISTAKE

Something happens to dear, old familiar waters between the closing of the last fishing season and the opening of the next. Rocks that we count on for stepping off the bank disappear. Overhanging trees that sheltered generations of fish go missing. The riverbed may have dropped a foot. The banks may have developed an undercut.

Winter storms and early season floods change the landscape of waterways everywhere. And the angler who steps into his old haunt for the first time may find himself without footing or in an unexpected hole.

THE FIX

Use caution when fishing in the spring even in water you knew very well the previous year and the year before that. High water from heavy storms may have scoured riverbeds, changing the makeup of your familiar fishing ground.

A wading staff helps improve balance and detect submerged rocks or deep holes.
Photo credit: Kat Rollin

Boulders, overhanging trees, stones, even the sand on the bed may have swept downstream, leaving one section deeper and pitted with holes and another full of new debris.

A wading staff is recommended for early-season fishing even for the most sure-footed wader.

Use it to prod for deep holes or hidden boulders that have been deposited by spring floods and to avoid stumbling over submerged rocks and logs that are invisible in the murky water of spring.

Be careful when approaching the water. Sodden banks that appear solid will give way unexpectedly with or without the weight of an angler standing on top.

Spring fly fishing is the epitome of the sport, perhaps because of the long-awaited opening of the season each year, perhaps because of the increasing abundance of insects as the season unfolds. Everything starts slowly. The fish are strong and healthy, but sluggish. The insects take their time to emerge. Anglers are tentative when first stepping into the water. But then, as temperatures warm and confidence returns, fishing heats up. Activity on the water increases with a bonanza of hatches, as clouds of emerging insects burst like the finale of a fireworks display, signalling the end of the spring season.

FISHING CONDITIONS

Spring comes to each region at a different date. The southern states see it first as the weather turns mild. Northern and mountainous regions experience spring later in the year, after the sun has moved close enough to the earth to heat the water and the ground. An angler in Tennessee can fish the early spring hatches, travel to Pennsylvania to fish them again, and use the same fly box a few weeks later in Montana and in the California Rockies.

In the early part of the season, the weather is usually just beginning to change, and the wintry chill is warmed daily by a few hours of sun. Water conditions vary with each river. The water temperatures may be in the 40s, and the air temperature can rise during the day from the 30s to the 50s and even the 60s and the 70s.

Spring rains and snowmelt keep waters high and cloudy.

In the first part of the season, the water temperature is cold and doesn't begin to warm until the early afternoon. Insects become active and the fishing productive. Anglers can fish in the morning hours without a hook-up and then watch the water come alive with hatches a couple of hours later.

Mountain streams swell with snowmelt and spring rains.

The best part of the season can be the early weeks before warm weather brings other outdoor enthusiasts to the rivers and woods. Early-season fly fishing yields an abundance of stocked fish released into waters by state or private organizations, solid numbers of holdover fish in certain waters, and a thriving population of wild fish in others.

WHERE THE FISH ARE

In the early season, when rivers are running cold and high, fish usually rest in slow water, out of the main current. Cold water temperatures cause a sluggish state of inactivity in fish. Predictably, they settle in spots that require less use of energy to exist. The high water and fast currents of spring reduce the number of sheltered areas for fish. An early season angler fishing with a dry fly should cast along the banks or at the tails of pools.

For the most part, fish stay deep in the early part of the season, feeding almost exclusively under the surface. The heavy water flows compel fish to remain at the bottom and not fight the currents while rising to the surface.

Most importantly, there is an abundance of subsurface insects drifting in the water. Some of the insects are preparing to transform to their next physical stage. Others are drifting in the water, having been dislodged prematurely by the current or as part of the behavioral drift that is Mother Nature's way of distributing the number of insects evenly in a stream. Those larvae let loose of their hold to drift to a less populated area in the stream. There are so many choices for a nymph fisherman in early spring.

Dry fly fishing can be productive, too, even on a breezy day in the early season. Recently emerged duns will be blown toward riverbanks before their wings are dry enough to fly away. The slow-moving trout need only pluck the insects from the surface without venturing into faster current.

FISHING TECHNIQUES

If you're planning to fish on the surface, you can begin your day on the stream as late as the afternoon after allowing the sun to warm the water's surface and stir the insect life. In spring, fish don't rise regularly to a fly until the water temperature reaches 51 degrees Fahrenheit.

When the water is high, cast from the safety of the shore to sheltered areas along the bank (A).

Be alert when fishing a dry fly in early spring: The flies are dark and hard to see against the dark water. The takes are not aggressive, but rather are almost delicate until the water temperatures warm enough to invigorate the fish.

In the typically high-water conditions of spring, you can also successfully fish nymphs and dry flies from the safety of the bank.

Fishing so close to shore requires only short casts, which eliminates the concern of back casts getting caught in overhanging branches. This is the time for the roll cast and bow-and-arrow cast, described in Chapter 5.

Fish do not spook as easily when feeding in the spring. Water temperatures warming from winter levels speed up their metabolism and the fish focus on replenishing their winter-wasted reserves. Your leader can be a manageable nine feet long for spring fishing on the surface (even shorter for water that is fast or cloudy, or for fishing under the surface).

When fishing nymphs with a downstream presentation, let the fly rise to the surface on the swing at the end of the drift. Give a couple of tugs on the

Good fishing techniques landed this prize brown trout. Photo credit: Marcelo Widman, Rio Monso Lodge, Patagonia, Argentina

line as the fly nears the surface. This action changes the fly's characteristics from an immature insect to one that is transforming to an adult and emerging from underwater.

The same strategy should be used when you are fishing upstream of your position. Cast your nymph upstream of the area where you expect a fish to be holding. Throw slack onto the water upstream of the fly, either with an upstream mend or a reach cast (see Chapter 9). When you anticipate that the fly has drifted to the fish, raise your rod tip in the air, angling it in the upstream direction to pull the fly to the surface in the fish's field of vision.

Streamers should be drifted with no action at first, and then fished with slow retrieves to imitate the sluggish metabolism of minnows swimming in cold water.

Later in the season, after the water has warmed, fish will become more aggressive when hitting flies on the surface. They swim to the upper levels of a water column with force to fight through the fast currents of spring waters. The energy brings them to a fly with what seems like an aggressive attack. This behavior calls for a heavier tippet to avoid the fly breaking off immediately on the take.

INSECTS AND FLIES

Early-season insect activity is standard on hatch charts in most regions. The corresponding flies—Quill Gordons, Hendricksons, Red Quills, Blue-Winged Olives, and March Browns are present in typical order, as are Dark Winter Caddis and Yellow Stoneflies.

The most dramatic change to your equipment happens in your fly box at this time of year. You'll typically begin the season using small, dark flies. As the weeks pass, your selections will become lighter in color and larger in size. By the end of the spring, your fly box should contain Sulphurs, Cahills, Drakes, and Golden Stoneflies. You should also carry a wide selection of nymphs—from small, dark flies to large ones—ready to imitate any of the subsurface insects that are drifting in the current.

SAFETY

Especially in the early part of the season, when the water and air can be extremely cold, it makes sense to layer your clothing.

GUIDE TIP

When fish are rising steadily, but refusing the active insect listed on the local fly shop wall, study the surface of the water carefully, looking for spinners. Temperature fluctuations in spring can affect the timing of a spinner fall, pushing it from evening to morning and even hours later, when least expected. If fish are nosing at the surface, tie on a spent spinner and float it with a dead drift.

A rain jacket will keep you warm when the weather is windy and dry when it's wet.

When the water is high, cast from the shore, and let your fly drift along the bank in the slower water.

The base layer—the first layer you put on—can be thin and should be of a material that will wick moisture and perspiration away from your skin, so as to avoid a chill and keep you warm. The mid-layer should be one that provides warmth while also drawing moisture farther away from you. The outer layer should protect you from the outside elements: wind and water.

When fishing rivers that are swollen in the spring, stand close to the shore where currents run more slowly or, even better, cast from the shore to the near water. The fish will often be in slower, more sheltered water.

FISHING ATTIRE

For your own comfort, wear warm layers under your waders, but leave plenty of room for movement and breathability, especially in your boots. Too many socks will constrict foot space, hamper circulation, and may cause your feet to cramp or become cold. It is best to wear a pair of thick wool socks with a thin layer that wicks moisture underneath.

CHAPTER 14

SUMMER FLY FISHING

Every year, the fishing club held its summer outing on the Farmington River in Connecticut. With water flowing from the depths of an upstream reservoir, this coldwater tail release provides the perfect conditions for midsummer trout fishing. Water temperatures remain in the upper 50s into August, keeping anglers in fleece and long underwear from the waist down, even while hardy float tubers drift by in bathing suits. Despite the description of the river, each year new members of the club come to the outing prepared for a different version of summer fishing: wet wading. I remember one youthful angler who stripped down to long underwear and swimming trunks in preparation for his first day on the Farmington. "This isn't California," he was told. He shook off the warnings, intent on showing the Easterners what a real angler wears in the summer. It wasn't long before he stumbled out of the water, teeth chattering under blue lips. Ninety-degree air temperatures and a hot sun soon warmed the angler enough to elicit a sheepish smile. We all noticed that he wore his waders the following year.

A COMMON MISTAKE

There are many anglers who continue to use the same equipment and fishing techniques throughout the year, regardless of the environment. An angler who fishes a hi-tech long-distance fly line all spring may not be concerned with its thickness and weight until he tries to cast onto the low, clear water of summer. The line, its shadow, the splash it makes are all elements that may spook fish.

THE FIX

Observe the conditions of the water before fishing in the summer. This cannot be said enough for every season. Grab an appropriate rod and corresponding fly line. After the snowmelt and final spring showers have left the

Fish the cool hours of evening, even into dark on familiar waters.

rivers, and the waters have subsided to calmer currents, an angler should fish with more delicate presentations on lighter equipment.

There is plenty of quality fishing available during the warmer months.

Many anglers fish for trout in tailwater rivers or in spring creeks, which maintain a cool temperature all season. Other anglers may switch and fish for warmwater species instead of trout. A bass at the end of your line is a powerful force with lots of muscle. Saltwater fishing is another great alternative to angling in a stream. Even a schoolie (a younger fish) is bigger than most of what one catches in freshwater.

WHERE THE FISH ARE

In the early part of the summer, before the water becomes too warm, trout will be found near the surface feeding on terrestrials and the last of the major emerging mayflies. They will be on the slow side of the seam between two currents, in positions where they can reach shelter quickly as needed: overhanging banks, submerged logs, large rocks, even a depth of three feet of water.

Bass will be found in vegetation and near structure. The vegetation offers both food and shelter to the fish. Most structures will do the same.

It is so important to take the temperature of the water before you fish.

Bass, panfish, and carp are all warmwater creatures that can tolerate being hooked and played in high water temperatures.

If the water is a trout fishery and its temperature is above 72 degrees Fahrenheit, find something else to do instead of fish. As water gets warmer, it holds less oxygen. Hooking and playing a trout in 75-degree water may actually suffocate it.

Trout will move to colder, more oxygenated water as the summer heats up. Look for springs and feeder streams, shaded areas, and fast, broken water:

In summer, look for fish in shaded water and other cold sections of a river.

all sections of a river that will provide more oxygen to the fish. As long as the temperatures are not unbearably warm (for the fish, not the angler) and you don't find trout packed together gasping for oxygen, you can proceed. At the same time, make sure that you are not fishing in an area that is a thermal refuge. Sections of rivers in many states have been designated thermal refuges for fish during the warmest weeks of summer. These are the sections to which trout migrate for cooler or more oxygenated water. If the area is not posted as a thermal refuge, but your thermometer indicates that it is, leave the fish alone and return another time. There is no sport in catching fish stressed by low oxygen in warm water.

FISHING CONDITIONS

Depending on the type of water, fishing in summer conditions can bring very different experiences. Wooded streams or spring creeks are just beginning to peak as the water temperatures rise. Large rivers or open streams with rocks eventually become warm and low.

Streams at a high elevation or protected from the sun by tree cover are too cold in the spring for fish activity. They warm with the summer heat, which means that fish will feed on the insects that have become active.

Water levels drop in the summer. The sun warms the water, but most importantly, it warms the rocks at the water's surface or just below it. The rocks retain the heat and cause the water temperature to rise. As the summer progresses, the rivers heat up, and fishing activity is affected.

On bright, sunny days, most of the feeding activity is subsurface, but you can still find success with dry flies. Fish continue to take flies off the surface just with less energy than in the rush of the spring. In summer, the fish are not fighting heavy currents and need only to nudge their mouths to the surface to take in a fly.

FISHING TECHNIQUES

In the dog days of summer, freshwater fishing slows to match the heat, the smooth current, and the general laze of the fishing day.

With lower levels and clearer water in summer rivers, anglers need to use stealth and patience to catch fish. Sunfish will still rise to anything that is thrown at them, and bass will chase a big streamer. But, a trout will take the time to examine a fly before biting or refusing.

Presentation is key to successful dry-fly fishing.

Presentation is key to successful dry-fly fishing. The fly must sit naturally in the water, float realistically downstream, dead drift, or skitter like its natural cousins.

Stalking a rising fish in a long, slow pool requires patience and stealth. When approaching a fishing spot in clear, slow, low water, wade gently without shuffling your feet on the river bottom or creating waves against your legs. When you reach your target spot, stop moving and let the water settle, the rings dissipate, and the calm return. Use this time to tie on your fly and study the water. Really look at it—the surface and below—to pinpoint feeding fish, current seams, and active insects. There is no need to hurry: If the fish is not spooked, it will continue to eat. As exciting as a rising fish is, a hooked one is even more so. Use long, small-gauge leaders, especially with tiny flies. If a fish is hovering near the surface, sipping flies, you need to cast only a few feet upstream of the dimple. If you can see a fish working and notice that it is following natural insects downstream for a distance before taking them, then you must cast farther upstream. Your presentation should be gentle, and your float should be a dead drift. Natural insects do indeed flutter on the surface, but especially with very small flies, it is fairly impossible to imitate the movement without disturbing the water with your leader.

Correct for drag even if you can't see it. Although rivers run more slowly at this time of year, there are probably still a number of currents between you and your fly. Crystal-clear water allows the fish to see with bionic eyes, and just a little drag can ruin your entire presentation. Throw extra slack into your cast. Mend upstream or downstream as needed to eliminate the current's pull on your fly. Hold your rod high, as you would when high-sticking a nymph, to keep your line out of difficult currents close to you.

GUIDE TIP

If you have difficulty controlling the slack in your cast, move to a different position. Your line may be floating through tricky current and can be controlled better from another casting angle.

In clear or slow water, try tying your fly onto a tippet that is one size smaller than what is called for. In other words, unless you are fishing bushy or heavy flies, use 6x on a size 16 Sulphur or 7x on a size 18 Griffith's Gnat. This will help cut the visibility of the tippet and of any drag it may create. This would be the time to make use of the Guide Tip in Chapter 4, which suggests a way to avoid a heavy fly twisting your light tippet.

Add extra length to your leader. With the exception of terrestrials, most flies are smaller in the summer, so the smaller diameter of your tippet makes sense.

When you set the hook, remember that you have on a light tippet, so don't haul back hard on your line and break off the fish. It actually requires very little effort to set the hook of a small fly. And your softer rod and lighter drag will help you fight the fish more effectively.

When water levels become lower and the clarity finer, you will notice that fish will take more time to examine your fly, even following it down-stream before hitting it. The finer-diameter tippet will help, but you must pay attention to drag. If you can see your fly dragging, the fish will ignore it. If you even *think* the fly might be dragging, be assured that the fish will have already noticed it. Throw extra slack into the line. Use your reach cast, S-cast—anything that will give your fly a drag-free float. Try to mend your line in the air before it hits the water. If you can master a cast that controls slack in the air, you won't risk ripping the water with your upstream mend.

Fish will feed on insects drifting in the line of bubbles, on the far side of the stream in this picture.

As the water level drops in a stream, the main current becomes even more important.

Look for the bubbles or detritus floating in a line down the river. Fish will position themselves under that line to feed on whatever is being carried downstream.

Try to bring your fish in as quickly as possible, so you don't tire it unnecessarily. When releasing the fish, practice good catch-and-release techniques. Keep the tired fish out of a very fast current, but do make sure that the water is moving enough to revive it. It may take longer to revive a fish in warm water, so stay with it. When the fish has regained its strength, it will swim away.

INSECTS AND FLIES

Summer fly fishing provides opportunities for anglers with every fly preference. On the surface, you will find large and small terrestrials, occasional large mayflies, and hatches of the smallest insects. Underwater, there are all the corresponding nymphs for the aquatic insects of summer as well as for the larger fall species that may become active early. Summer is also a good season for fishing streamers to mimic minnows, leeches, and sculpins.

The most prevalent of the surface aquatic insects in summer are tiny Blue-Winged Olives, Tricos, and Caddis.

Although active all year, terrestrials abound in the summertime. Non-aquatic insects that are blown into the water and eaten by fish include ants, beetles, and grasshoppers. Large terrestrials such as hoppers appear when the morning sun has warmed the vegetation, especially on hot, windy days. Fish them like the landlubbers they are. Drop the artificial with a soft plop onto the water under trees or brush. Let it sit motionless for a few seconds, then twitch the fly as if it were struggling for footing. In a current, terrestrials will sink into the film layer of the water and become trapped, unable to move, after its initial struggle. Have fun with terrestrials. They are candy to a trout.

A twitch is easily achieved with a slight downstream cast. At the end of your cast, keep your rod tip high and your fly line upstream of the fly. After the fly lands on the water, move the rod tip sharply, so that the fly jumps upstream an inch. Lower the rod tip slowly to allow the fly to dead-drift several feet. At the end of the drift, give a sharp tug on the line to twitch the fly again, pulling it under the surface.

The best place to fish grasshoppers is along the bank, especially undercut or grass-lined banks. Trout will swim out of their feeding lanes to go after a hopper and may follow a fly as far as twenty feet before taking it.

Grasshoppers are large insects that struggle in the water, but ants and small beetles get caught in the meniscus (film layer) and cannot move. Their imitations should be dead-drifted, without twitching or other movement. Beetles are active all day, from early morning through dark, and are found on the water more often on windy days. The larger flies can be presented with subtle twitches, but flies size 18 and smaller should float motionless.

Ants should be fished with the same techniques as beetles, but with an even softer landing on the water. Ants are especially effective when trout are easily spooked. There is a frenzied early morning appearance of ants in the summer, but you will also find ants in the soft, warm, late afternoons. Float your imitation low in the film with a dead drift.

> ## GUIDE TIP
>
> Terrestrials lack buoyancy, often submerging after landing on the water. Let the fly sink as it floats, and don't dry it before casting again.

No one pounds up a fish, but that's the phrase used to describe an angler causing a fish to rise after countless casts. The best fly to use when there is nothing to match is an attractor. Attractor patterns do not imitate specific naturals, but can be mistaken for various insects. The Yellow Humpy, Ausable Wulff, and Elk-Hair Caddis all have shapes that can resemble that of a caddis, a mayfly, or even a beetle. A Stimulator's silhouette is like that of a stonefly or a grasshopper. Attractor dry flies should float well and be easily visible in all water and light conditions. They should be large enough to draw a trout to the surface, but not larger than the biggest natural that is active at the time. Fish attractors in fast water where a hesitating trout would lose its meal. Select an attractor pattern because it was recommended by a local, because it matches what you find in the bushes, or because you like it. The choice is serendipitous and the take, therefore, is immensely rewarding

FISHING ATTIRE

Temperature affects the angler as well as the fish. When the air temperature warms up, many fly fishers think of wet wading: fishing in shorts and boots, without waders. Think twice before you make the decision to wet-wade. Consider the land you will cross on your way to the stream. Poison ivy, deer ticks, nettles, and other irritants become hazards when you walk through the woods with bare skin exposed. And once you get into the water, you have other concerns. Cool streams feel great on a warm summer day, but standing in chilly water for hours, even in the hot sun, will cause your body temperature to drop, possibly exposing you to hypothermia even on a very warm day. This sounds overly cautious, I know, but it's important to weigh the potential consequences of every option before choosing your fishing style.

Even though the air temperature can be beastly warm in summer, anglers should dress for the water temperature. Wear lightweight clothing on the upper half of your body, and protect your skin from sun with long sleeves, suntan lotion, and a hat. At the same time, consider the temperature of the water you will be in when dressing your lower half. It may seem absurd, but you will be very comfortable wearing long underwear and fleece if you're fishing below a dam. Trust me, standing in a cold tailwater is not much fun if you are underdressed.

CHAPTER 15

AUTUMN FLY FISHING

The weather forecast called for unseasonable warmth in early November. "Let's go fishing," suggested a friend. We gathered our gear and took off for the day. There was little activity when we arrived at the river: It was the middle of the week, and there were no other fishermen around. The day was still, and the water level was low and inviting: easy to enter, easy to wade. There were no insects buzzing the surface or fish rising to feed. My friend and I waded into one of my favorite pools and moved to the positions we habitually use to approach this water. I fished the surface with dry flies for a while, hoping to entice an alert brown trout to the top. As the day lengthened, I tied on a streamer, admitting that the fish were hunkered down in the depths for the season. After a few hours, we caught three fish between the two of us: a couple of smaller brown trout and a stunning rainbow—fat and long—measuring twenty-one inches from nose to tail.

"What was wrong today?" my fishing buddy asked. Nothing, he and I decided. It had been a beautiful day, with weather conditions stolen from an earlier month. But, this was not spring fishing. The warmth of the sun, although appreciated, had done little for the fishing activity under the surface. Even so, we had caught fish in a secluded pool on a beautiful day in November.

Autumn fishing is a distillation of all the properties that make up the sport. The water is low and clear. The insect population has thinned out. The current is moving with a purpose. The river has a limited time to get where it's going before the cold weather settles in and ice stops all movement. The fish, too, are in a no-nonsense mood, feeding seriously to fatten themselves for the winter months. Every instant is valuable, precious time not to be wasted.

Autumn days *feel* shorter. The sun may be warm, but there are fewer daylight hours, so the air cools down faster. Cool air. Cool water tempera-

Clear water reflects colors of the foliage.

tures. The weather conditions affect the hatches, which are less abundant in the fall. The fish are also affected: Brown trout, brook trout, and most salmon go into their spawning periods. Their colors become richer and their nature more aggressive. They will be territorial and attack minnows and leeches invading their space. Streamers are not safe from these fierce fish. Tie them onto a heavy tippet and retrieve them with gusto. The fish are also bulking up, building up extra layers before their metabolism slows as the water temperature cools. Suddenly, that skinny little Olive looks very appetizing and the fat Isonychia even more so.

With fewer anglers and recreational boaters, you will have more water to cast to. With fewer insects hatching, you will have hungrier trout. The equation should end with more fish on the line. But, this is fishing. There will still be times when you don't hook up. That's why Mother Nature invented leaves and decreed that they fall from trees in autumn. Leaves float down a stream and snag on hooks. Many an unsuspecting fly fisher mistakes the tug of a maple leaf for the bite of a rainbow. It's a thrill, and you should enjoy it while it lasts.

WHERE THE FISH ARE

What do fish do in the fall? They retreat to deeper, darker, more protected areas and will stay there through winter. Protected by the depth and slower currents, fish have more time to inspect their food options and expend less energy doing so. Fish rise to the surface in colder water during autumn more than they do in spring. In the early season, they won't begin to rise until the water reaches a temperature of 51 degrees Fahrenheit. In the fall, they will rise to dry flies when the water is in the low 40s, even the high 30s.

When it's cold and clear, you will find that fish tend to hang out in pods. There will be a bunch of fish positioned in one area, sometimes only one spot in an entire stretch of water. When you've found a fishy spot, or even if you

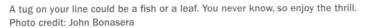

A tug on your line could be a fish or a leaf. You never know, so enjoy the thrill.
Photo credit: John Bonasera

just think it might be the right place, make sure that you fish the water carefully. If you see a fish and it ignores your fly, don't pull the fly up sharply. Remember that just behind or next to the fish you've seen may be another one or two, or three, one of which may want your fly.

FISHING TECHNIQUES

To enjoy autumn fishing, an angler must change tactics on the water, pay attention to details, and work with precision. In other words, everything counts.

As in the low waters of summer, when approaching a fishing spot, wade slowly and quietly toward a fish. When you reach your desired position, stop all movement to allow the rippled water to settle and the fish to resume its feeding.

Autumn fishing requires concentration: The flies are small and the takes subtle. The water is clear, and often the light is bright, giving the advantage to the fish. The indications of a strike at this time of year are often very slight. If your fly or strike indicator disappears, or the water wrinkles, set the hook.

If you are fishing dry flies, cast, as always, to the fish rising closest to you. If there is no rise, begin with the near waters, seams, and bubble lines, eventually working to those elements that are farther away. Long casts can disturb the water and put down fish. They will start to feed again, in their own time, not yours.

Flies are even more visible in the clear water of autumn, which means that fish notice an unnatural float and immediately bypass your fly for a living, tasty morsel. Now, more than ever, it is important to throw slack in your cast to ensure a longer natural drift.

When fishing downstream, throw as much slack as possible into your cast. Just as in summer, use specialty casts for aerial mending.

Remember that it is more effective, especially when there is slack in the line, to set the hook by keeping the rod close to the water and moving its tip in a plane parallel to the surface. The friction of the line sliding through the water away from the fish will help set the hook more successfully than the effort of pulling the rod and raising it high above your head in an attempt to eliminate extra line.

Cast your streamer across the water, but slightly upstream of your position. Let the fly sink as it drifts downstream. The first seconds will find the fly wiggling around and down in the current as it sinks, like a wounded fish drifting with the current. Then, as the line tightens, the fly looks alive and takes on a swimming action against the current as it swings around in an arc.

Drift nymphs deep in the water. To get them down, pinch split-shot onto the leader eight inches to a foot above the fly. This will allow the fly a more natural movement.

If the water is cold enough to make fish sluggish, it is cold enough to slow aquatic insects and baitfish as well. Keep your flies out of the main current. Let them drift down the edges or sit in slow water. Fish nymphs with a dead drift and, when you use an active retrieve with a streamer, make it a slow one.

To soften the effect of your back cast, retrieve the line by drawing it in gently through the water before making another cast. Bring it out of the water quietly without ripping the surface. Lift your arm until only the leader remains in the water before beginning the swift acceleration of your back cast. On your forward cast, allow the line to open completely before lowering your rod in a controlled manner, dropping the fly line lightly onto the surface. In other words, practice good presentation techniques.

GUIDE TIP

Fish the cast you lay down, even if it's not the one you wanted. You can correct the placement of the fly on your next cast.

SPAWNING FISH AND OTHER CHARACTERS

A number of fish spawn in the autumn, such as brown trout, brook trout, and salmon. Most salmon don't feed actively during spawning, but a fish will lash out at a fly that bothers it or invades its spawning bed. Trout feed actively before and after spawning, and they will also attack a fly that is bothersome. If you spot a spawning fish, do the ethically correct thing and leave it alone. Stay away from known redds or spawning beds. But, if you should hook a spawner, expect a fierce take from a short-tempered fish protecting its territory.

In addition to the fish carefully examining every fly, there are crazy bruisers cruising the water looking for trouble. Acting more like sharks than freshwater species, these fish slice through the current and attack anything in their way. Large streamers retrieved quickly or at erratic rates annoy these cannibals enough to cause chase. It is great fun to upset these monsters and bring them in using a mouthful of marabou. My favorite streamers at this time of year are Conehead Yellow Muddlers, Mickey Finns, and white Woolly Buggers. Cast one across or slightly downstream, let it sink a few seconds, and then strip it in. If you are aiming for a particular cruising fish, anticipate where it will next appear, cast beyond its path, and retrieve your offering as a scared minnow trying to get away from a bullying enemy. Try not to retrieve your fly so that it chases the fish: There is nothing more unnatural than a skinny little minnow attacking a giant trout.

INSECTS AND FLIES

The aquatic insects that are active in autumn are Caddis, Olives, Tricos (in the morning), Baetis (in the afternoon), and Isonychia—the largest insect out there at this time.

Your autumn fly boxes should be filled with attractor patterns such as Red Humpies; terrestrials, especially crickets and ants; scuds; leeches; and orange, red, and yellow streamers. Your dries should include small Blue-Winged Olive duns, Tricos, Baetis (a CDC emerger in 18 and 20), Slate Drakes in 14, and Caddis in green, brown, and tan. The soft hackle of your wet flies may resemble emerging Caddis, so carry some of them in green, brown, and tan as well. And, you should also have plenty of Beadhead Pheasant Tail and Hare's Ear nymphs.

Under low light conditions, use patterns that have tinsel or gold ribbing. On bright, sunny days, choose brightly colored patterns, especially with red: Royal Wulffs, Royal Coachmen, Trudes, and flies tied with peacock herl to catch the light.

If you tie your own flies, use bright colors such as pink or yellow for the posts, making the flies much easier to see in low water and foam.

FISHING ATTIRE

As for clothing, bring layers. The air may be warm in the middle of the day, but remember that there are fewer hours of sun and, as it begins to set, the air can become brisk. It can rain a lot in the autumn, with fronts moving in quickly. No matter what the weatherman says, carry a rain jacket. A cold and wet angler can experience hypothermia all too quickly.

Layer clothing
designed for
standing outside in
cold temperatures.

The key to dressing is to layer wisely. Certainly, people have been fishing in cooler months for years without harm. But nowadays, anglers can fish
wearing clothing that has been designed for every condition. Make sure that
the clothing you buy for autumn fishing was intended for standing outside in
cold temperatures and not running, biking, skiing, or any other very active
sport. Different activities require different clothing. Look for hunters' clothing; they sit in duck blinds and tree stands for hours on end. Much as I like to
think that we are burning off millions of calories when we fly fish, it is prudent
to gear up for a more sedentary sport. Cotton is not a good choice in any
season, especially next to the skin. It doesn't keep you warm, and it holds

Wear a large, bright patch of safety color.

moisture, which, in turn, will chill you. Your base layers should keep you warm and wick moisture away from your skin.

Socks are extremely important. Rather than wear two heavy pairs, layer with a thin micropoly liner next to your skin and a thicker wool pair on top. The micropoly will wick the moisture away from your feet, and the wool will keep you warm. Wool is great. It has oils that will keep you warm even when it's wet. I wear two pairs of cashmere socks, which are thinner than regular wool and keep me perfectly comfortable.

Drink water. You may not think you're sweating in the cooler temperatures, but you are, as evidenced by the dampness around your knees at the end of the day.

Finally, consider wearing an orange or red hat in the fall. There are many hunting seasons going on at this time of year. Hunting accidents don't happen just on land. Anglers fishing near riverbanks have been peppered with buckshot spray. For safety's sake, it's best to wear a large, bright patch of color and to let any hunters in the area know that you are there.

Don't miss out on autumn fly fishing. Keep your rods out and your gear by the door. Steal away whenever you can. Get out there and fish. It couldn't be better. It couldn't be prettier. It couldn't be shorter. Catch it while it's there to catch.

CHAPTER 16

WINTER FLY FISHING

To fly fish for steelhead on the Douglaston Salmon Run in Pulaski, New York, anglers dress in the middle of the night to get to the river fifteen minutes before sun-up, just to guarantee their places on the water. By early afternoon, the frigid air and lack of sleep have stupefied many of them.

I was fishing the Douglaston Run on just such a day a few years ago. My friend, Peter, also a guide, was nearby with a female client. As I watched, she cast over and over again, trying in vain to shoot enough line to reach the plunge pool eight feet below where she and Peter were standing. "For some reason, I can't get my line out," she complained. "Your guide's freezing," Peter replied. His comment did not get a response from his client. A moment of silence passed, then she restated her problem. "I'm having difficulty getting the line out." Peter repeated his earlier comment. "Your guide's freezing," he said. As I watched, she turned to him, obviously annoyed that he was grumbling about his own discomfort. Before she could say anything, Peter, realizing that she thought he was complaining about the cold, quickly spoke up and pointed to her fly rod: "No, no, your *guides* are frozen." Sure enough, the guides on her rod were iced up, preventing the line from shooting out.

A quick dip of the rod into the water, with a temperature warmer than the air, provided a temporary fix.

A COMMON MISTAKE

Not all anglers are driven to cast into cold, wintry waters, but those who are share the same problem in attaching their flies. It is extremely difficult to tie tiny flies onto a thin tippet in the middle of winter. Cold hands are not nimble, nor are hands clad in thick gloves. Whatever the attire for their hands, winter anglers in cold climates will agree that knots, a fine tippet, and little flies do not assemble well when tied by frozen fingers.

A steelhead on your line is the ultimate winter freshwater fly-fishing experience. The fish rocket through the water and jump several times before being netted. Photo credit: Joseph Ceballos

THE FIX

Tiny flies and a small-gauge tippet are difficult to work with under ideal conditions. When the air temperature hovers just above freezing, it is frustrating to impossible to tie knots with cold fingers. To reduce the number of knots you have to tie when on the water in the winter, pre-tie lengths of tippet to a number of flies you anticipate using. Wrap the tippet and fly around a rectangular piece of cardboard that has been notched on each side with one-third-inch slits. Secure the lengths of tippet in the slits, and you'll be able to keep your flies and tippets neat and tangle-free. When you get to the stream, you will find it much easier to tie one surgeon's knot to attach the tippet-fly combination.

Winter fly fishing in a river is stimulating. Your senses are challenged by frigid air and water temperatures, the shocking glare of the sun off snow, ice, and water, the sharpness of sound cutting through winter silence, and the smell of dampness in the air and on the ground.

Winter fly fishing: a great way to get out and enjoy uncrowded water. Photo Credit: Joseph Ceballos

WHERE THE FISH ARE

Fish retreat to deeper, darker, more protected areas and will stay there through the winter. Fish continue to eat, but do not need to take in as many calories because they are expending fewer by slowing down and moving around less.

Fish also migrate to warmer water. They will leave small feeder streams, swimming downstream to spend the cold season in main branches of rivers, where the water is deeper and does not freeze.

FISHING TECHNIQUES

The metabolism of a fish slows down in the cold, allowing it to survive the winter conditions. Your reactions also have to be slower. Give the fish time to really take that hook before setting it.

Protected by the depth and slower currents, the fish have more time to inspect their food options and expend less energy doing so. Takes can be subtle: a gentle, but definite tug on the line or nothing at all. The natural bait you are imitating with your fly is also sluggish in the cold.

Fish Woolly Buggers and streamers with a slower retrieve than you would use in warmer water. Insects as well as fish are sluggish in the cold water. Streamers should be fished in slow water, down near the bottom. Just like the larger fish, bait fish stay out of heavy current and in warmer water.

Drop nymphs deep, and fish them with a dead drift. To get to the bottom, keep adding weight to your leader until you feel your nymph ticking along the riverbed.

Use small flies and a lighter tippet for dry fly fishing. Water is usually crystal clear in the winter, making presentation and drag-free drifts critical. Most of the dry-fly activity will be in the middle of a river where the water is warmer because of its depth.

GUIDE TIP

When winter fishing with dry flies, cast toward the riverbanks if there is an ice shelf. Don't ignore these areas where fish will hang out waiting for little stoneflies to blow into the water.

When choosing your fishing equipment for a winter day, use the same reasoning you would in the height of the season. A stiffer rod will cast large streamers, heavily weighted nymphs, even wet flies. It will cut through a breeze and play strong fish. But, if you are fishing smaller dry flies on a tiny tippet, you will want a rod that offers a more gentle presentation with a softer action and flexible tip that will yield to takes on a fine tippet.

Don't overplay a fish at this time of year. And, when you catch one, make a point of reviving it longer before releasing it back to the stream. This is because a river's current usually runs more slowly in winter and, with less tumbling, it carries less oxygen.

INSECTS AND FLIES

River conditions vary even within a climate zone, so the information here is simply a general overview. If you are fishing in the winter, as throughout the rest of the year, it is always best to consult the hatch chart of your local fly shop.

While bears hibernate snug in their caves, the less ferocious members of the animal kingdom continue to be active. Mayflies and caddis emerge from the river depths on schedule in the winter just as in the warmer seasons. You won't find the air thick with insects in a winter hatch, but you might see regattas of recently emerged insects floating on the surface. And the fish will eat the bugs wherever they are to be found—in the depths, just under the surface film, even on the surface.

Nymphs should be weighted to drop them through the water faster. Although you want a fair representation of basic imitations, have a few larger nymphs on hand. In the winter, a fish is more likely to move after a big fly that it recognizes, so as to get more food for the energy it expends in the chase. Stock up on Hare's Ear Nymphs, Pheasant Tails, Prince Nymphs, and Copper Johns to cover most of your needs. Then, add a few Kaufman Stoneflies to the mix.

For dry flies, keep a selection of small flies in your box: midges, small caddis, and Blue-Winged Olives, in sizes 18–22. It is always wise to have a few ants and beetles as well.

Your streamer wallet should be full of Woolly Buggers, Sculpins, and flies that are tied to imitate small fish, including Mickey Finns, Muddler Minnows, and Black-Nosed Dace.

> ## GUIDE TIP
> Use a Griffith's Gnat when there are midges on the water to mimic a group of them and to interest the fish that wisely selects a mouthful of food instead of picking off one little bite at a time.

FISHING LINES

In all but extreme cold temperatures, your choice of line is subjective, with personal preference being the most important factor. If you are fishing when the air temperature drops to freezing and the water is just above that, you should bring along lines that remain supple when cold. Again, this is for rarified situations, but you should be aware that some lines will twist or stiffen when fished in cold water. Smaller weights (2-, 3-, and 4-weight lines) have more memory, holding their coils more readily than larger (5-, 6-, and 7-weights). The lines remain usable, but casting becomes difficult.

FISHING ATTIRE

Your clothing concerns will be the same as for early spring and late autumn fishing, just a little more extreme. Remember your rain jacket or any jacket that will retain body warmth and protect you from the wind.

In some areas, winters are mild and require protection that is less excessive. Air temperatures can be warm in the middle of the day. Other climates are very cold, sometimes damp or windy. Dress accordingly and always in layers.

Lightweight, warm layers work best. As noted for the other cold seasons, the layer closest to your skin should be a base layer made of a material that wicks moisture away from your body. Do not use cotton. Remember the outdoor saying: Cotton kills. Layer two should be fleece or a similar material that will provide warmth. Layer three should provide protection from the weather, wind or wet.

Cover your extremities. Socks should be chosen for warmth and wicking. A warm hat will protect your head, where your body's warmth is most likely to escape. Wear polarized sunglasses to protect your eyes from the glare of the winter sun or snow reflecting on the water. Gloves are important, especially for the line hand, which tends to get wet. Fingerless fleece and thin wool work well and are not bulky. If you don't like to wear anything on your hands, keep some handwarmers in a pocket for quick warming.

My winter fishing uniform includes cashmere socks, long underwear, fleece top and bottom, a Patagonia puff vest, a scarf at my neck, and a windbreaker. A fleece band protects my ears and forehead, and thin wool fingerless gloves with heat packets inside cover my hands.

Pay particular attention to your feet. If they're cold or cramped, there's no way you're going to feel comfortable. Remember that tight boots, filled with too much wader, sock, and foot will hamper the circulation of blood in your feet and cause you to get cold. Some anglers like to put foot warmers in their boots for extra warmth as well.

Waders

Most waders are fine for any but the extreme conditions of winter. If you wear breathables, put at least two layers of clothing under the waders to provide a triple buffer between your skin and the water. Make sure your waders are large enough to accommodate this bulking up. Two layers of socks squeezed into neoprene stocking feet and then boots, with no space for air, will slow circulation, cause your feet to tingle, go numb, and then cold.

Neoprenes were made for cold-water fishing. Breathables offer an improved option, with your body warmth held in by the clothing you layer underneath.

If the current is heavy or the wading difficult, I wear my stockingfoot waders with heavy boots to feel secure in my wading. But, if the water is

Snow sticks to boot soles. Wear Korkers or spikes to avoid slipping. Photo credit: Joseph Ceballos

low or the river bed easy to navigate, the bootfoot is great because it allows a layer of air to act as insulation around your foot. This buffer layer is important for keeping an angler warm, so you can fish for a longer period of time.

Korkers are spiked overshoes that attach to the soles of wading boots. The spikes grind into ice to stabilize walking. If you are fishing in icy areas, even crossing an ice shelf to get to the water, attach Korkers or another similar device to your boots.

SAFETY

A wading staff is a vital piece of gear in winter. It will help improve your balance when you're walking across snow and ice, and it will allow you to prod the riverbed in front of you when wading in dark, murky water. A wading staff can save your life.

Move around to keep warm and increase blood circulation in your feet and legs. Don't stand in one place for too long.

If you get cold, get out of the water. The air is usually warmer than the water and will help raise your body temperature.

If you begin to shiver, stop fishing, and get out of the water. Take a break. The last thing you want to do is flirt with hypothermia because in the extreme, it can kill you.

If you feel a "pins and needles" sensation or numbness in your fingers or toes, stop fishing immediately. Frostbite is not fun. If you get it, your fingers will be affected even years later. Believe me.

Cold weather fishing is sublime—a blast of refreshing air, sharp as ice; a clear stream of molten crystal sparkling under a solid blue sky. Embrace it as you would a snowman: dressed warmly and for a limited length of time.

CHAPTER 17

WHEN ALL ELSE FAILS

There were two anglers in the boat. One was intent on catching a fish, working with everything he knew. The second was using the drift to relax in the sun. He threw out a line, let it sink, closed his eyes, and leaned back in his seat. The first angler continued to tie on new flies, present his casts, watch the feathers float on the surface, retrieve the flies, and cast again, over and over.

It was midday in the heat of the summer without any fish activity on the surface of the water. In fact, there was usually never any activity on the surface of the water here at any time because it was a small lake. Fish teemed below the surface, but were rarely seen rising to anything regularly. The active angler could not figure out how to attract the fish to his fly.

Suddenly, the resting angler's rod bowed down and, in the distance, a fish jumped clear of the water. It was a sizeable fish, one that seemed to be attached to the rod by the line that was now trailing off its jaw. The angler shouted and reeled in a three-pound smallmouth bass, proudly showing it to his now-deflated fishing buddy who reeled in his own line and admitted defeat for the day.

A COMMON MISTAKE

Many times a fly fisher will arrive at the water armed with basic information about the season's fishing activities, but not the most current information. Or, he or she may not be prepared at all.

Intent on enjoying a day on the water and not worried about being spot-on correct with his technique selections, the angler may ignore the clues around him indicating how to proceed with his fishing. Or, he may look around, but see nothing that would help.

It happens all too often that an angler will come to unknown water, a pool with the reputation of being a very fishable spot, and not know how to proceed.

THE FIX

An angler can feel overwhelmed at the first sight of what looks to be an ideal location. If there are no signs of fish or insects, tie on a streamer and work the water by casting across and slightly downstream with a short line, perhaps twenty feet. Cast the same length line and let the fly swing downstream three times, then lengthen your line by about a foot, and cast in the same direction with a complete swing downstream for another three tries Lengthen your line again and follow the same procedure until you have cast as far as you can. Next move downstream two to three feet, and cast the full length of line three times, again allowing the line to swing downstream before pulling up for your next cast. With this technique, you will cover a lot of water in your search for fish.

Swinging a streamer is an effective way to find fish, like this healthy brown trout, in unfamiliar waters.

In winter, use a heavy streamer or weight it to drop to the bottom of the river. Allow your fly to swing with a dead drift, mimicking the sluggish movement of small fish in cold temperatures.

In warmer seasons, use lightly weighted flies, which will drift higher in the water, and, after the first cast and swing, retrieve the fly by pulling in a little line, stopping to let it swing, then pulling in more line. Repeat this maneuver until the fly has swung directly downstream of your rod tip. The stripping action adds life to the fly and a second dimension to your presentation: dead drift and active swimming.

Swinging a streamer through a river is an effective way to raise fish and to cover unfamiliar water.

WHEN THE FISH DON'T RESPOND

If fish are not taking the insects that are hatching, switch to a pattern known to work in that area.

This wily rainbow trout responded to an Orange Stimulator plopped onto the foam line.

If fish are not responding to the flies suggested by a local authority, try some of these suggestions:

- It is wise to have several different patterns in your fly box to imitate nymphs, emergers, and adult insects of the active naturals. If the fish don't like the look of one style, they may key onto another.

- When natural imitations are not interesting the fish, tie on an attractor pattern.

- If hatch activity is not visible, try using attractor patters and terrestrials. Flies such as the Elk-Hair Caddis, Stimulator, Adams, and Woolly Bugger are excellent search patterns.

GUIDE TIP

Changing flies after six to ten casts should help you find a pattern that works.

A LOOSE ROD SECTION

Vigorous casting can loosen rod sections in their ferrules. A final cast may even send your rod tip sailing into the air, free from the rest of the rod. Don't panic. Most of the time your tip will land on the water and float downstream until it has reached the end of the fly line. If you have a fly tied onto the tippet, the hook will usually catch on the tiptop and prevent the rod tip from floating away. Gently pull in your line, retrieve the section of rod, and put it firmly back in place.

To prevent a section from separating from the rest of the rod, make it part of your routine to check the connections after catching each fish or tying on a new fly.

CHAPTER 18

FISHING WITH A GUIDE

The angler was on a business trip to Aspen, Colorado, but managed to schedule a morning of guided fishing between meetings. She arrived at the fly shop in need of equipment, a little embarrassed at having travelled unprepared. Feeling it necessary, she described her fishing skills and preference for using dry flies. Several hours later, she and her guide were fishing the Roaring Fork, a fly fisher's dream river. It was the middle of August, and the trout were not rising to the surface. Finally, after casting over and over with no sign of a fish, the angler admitted defeat and asked her guide for a subsurface fly. "But I didn't bring any nymphs," the guide stated. "You said you only like to fish dry flies." The day's fishing was immediately clouded by disappointment and anger: disappointment in the fishing experience and anger at the guide for not being prepared. This is my story. I was the angler and can attest that these two emotions colored the memory of that outing for the next ten years. What a waste.

THE MISTAKE

Hiring a fishing guide can be daunting. I can name several anglers with tales similar to mine, or who have complained about watching a guide catch trophy trout while they stand by fishless, or who have been left alone for hours when the guide disappeared. The number of horror stories is infinite. Something gets lost between the opening greeting in a telephone conversation and the final handshake at the end of the fishing day. The missing element is communication, and when it's not there, a perfectly planned getaway may turn into a disappointing day, the memories of which return only to kick an angler sharply.

THE FIX

To avoid any discomfort, you need to be honest with a potential guide when calling to make the initial contact: honest in your expectations of the guide and the fishing trip, and in your description of your fishing skills. Treat this phone call like an interview for a job, which is exactly what it is. You are looking to hire a professional for a temporary position. You have certain expectations of what you want the guide to do for the day. And you, in turn, need to provide the guide with information about yourself: your fishing experience and temperament. If the guide on the phone sounds like the person you need to fill the job, move on to logistical details: the guide's fee, what it covers, the length of the day, transportation, a cancellation policy, a reservation deposit, and the next communication.

Information that must be conveyed includes such things as:

- The kind of fishing you are seeking: fly fishing, wading or drifting in a boat, fish species.
- The type of guiding you anticipate: instructional, placement on the water and being left alone, or a bit of both.
- The experience you would like: a relaxing trip surrounded by beautiful scenery, a productive day in the best waters regardless of setting, a challenging fishing expedition designed to test your skills to the extreme, an exploration of new waters that would be useful for when you return without a guide.

In addition, ask the guide about his style and experience, whether or not he instructs during a typical fishing day, how long he has been fishing the particular water, if he is licensed (if the state requires it) and insured, and whether he provides equipment, if necessary.

Once you have established what you are looking for, put yourself in the picture: Are you a restless angler who can't stand still for more than three casts? An overworked executive looking for peace and quiet or a thrilling day to crowd out workday stress? A total novice hoping to learn a new sport or, if an experienced angler, what are your skill levels? Go through this same exercise describing your fishing partner, if you're inviting one.

To complete the picture, fill in the blanks with any needs and potentially disruptive points: Someone who can't swim *needs* to be concerned about wading safety, someone who is pregnant *needs* to take frequent bathroom breaks, someone who is on medication *needs* to stop to attend to his health, someone out of the office for a day may *need* to call in once or twice . . .

Outline the expectations you have of the guide. It's reasonable to expect the guide's attention for the duration of the day. And, even if you are not interested in fishing lessons, you may be open to suggestions for improving your fishing techniques or learning a new method on unfamiliar water. It is more than fair to confirm that the guide will not fish on your time.

Whatever you want, you can ask for. Whatever you ask for, as long as it's reasonable and you've asked in advance of the trip, you can have. The guide wants you to have a good day and be happy.

Most guides choose to be on the water not only because they love fishing, but also because they love taking other people fishing. The more informed a guide is in advance of your trip, the more prep work he can do, so that more time can be spent doing what you want on your actual fishing day.

Julia Bradford enjoys fishing Montana's Ruby River with her guide, Donna Tate McDonald.
Photo credit: Charles Warner

But if, in spite of all your communications in advance of the trip, you are unhappy or uncomfortable while you are fishing, speak up. Tell your guide immediately. If you're uncomfortable with the water, say so. If you want more instruction or less, say so. If you've chosen a good guide, he has probably prepared several backup plans as needed. Communicate early so you don't lose your day.

When you are on the stream, remember that the guide is a professional doing a service for you, but not your servant. Heed his caution and advice. You're paying for it. If you choose to do your own thing, that's fine. But remember, it was your decision.

Harry McVickar caught this six-pound rainbow trout with guide Hamp Cross on Frog Hollow Brook outside Helen, Georgia. Photo credit: Lansing McVickar

Too often, we think that because our guide is able to see fish through water and anticipate their moves, he is also superhuman and can see through us and read an angler's mind. This is simply not true, and a test for superhuman powers may just upset the angler, frustrate the guide, and lead to a disappointing day.

If, on the other hand, you communicate openly with your guide and listen to the advice and knowledge of the angling professional he is, you should be rewarded with a satisfying day.

A bull trout and fishing guide Jeremy Kehrein gave angler Kurt Huhner a great day on the Blackfoot River outside Missoula, Montana. Photo credit: Irene Huhner

GUIDE'S NOTE

Tipping

A gratuity always seems to be an awkward issue for both the angler and the guide. Although not required, it is customary to add a gratuity to the guide's fee for service well performed. When considering a gratuity, think of the service itself, not the number of fish caught, hooked, lost, or not even seen. There is no standard for tipping a guide, but I have found that, on average, outfitters suggest a gratuity of $50 per angler for a full day. With this in mind, consider what your guide has done or not done for you. Did you require any special efforts of the guide? Did he stay out longer than the contracted time? Did he save your life? Did he leave you in the middle of the stream and return an hour later to check on you? Did he move around the bend to fish himself? Was the guide prepared and professional? Did he meet your expectations and then surpass them?

If you were pleased with the guide services, tip enough to show it. If you were not pleased, do not feel obligated to provide a gratuity. I have been on the receiving end of both: the extreme examples being one client who tips $100 for every fish he catches and another who tips only if he lands a fish regardless of the number that rise to his fly.

Remember, a guide can only lead you to the fish. It is up to you to set the hook and reel the fish in.

CHAPTER 19

STREAM ETIQUETTE

L ee Wulff Run on Willowemoc Creek just outside the Catskill Fly Fishing Center and Museum, in Livingston Manor, New York, is a peaceful section of river that is steeped in tradition and history. It is also a favorite spot for the trout-stocking truck, which makes it a popular run with fly fishers. One day while introducing a new angler to the Willow, I witnessed the classic breach of stream etiquette.

The river is fifty feet wide with a dense foliage backdrop in this part of the run. Two anglers were fishing from the same bank about seventy-five yards apart. With a bend in the bank, the anglers could not see each other, but from my vantage point directly across the water, I had a perfect view of the scene. The downstream angler was working his way upstream, casting to rises above him before taking a few steps and casting again. The second angler was farther upstream and hidden by overhanging brush on both sides. He was forced to roll-cast upstream. When the downstream angler had waded to within a dozen feet of his upstream counterpart, the two anglers finally noticed each other. The downstream angler, who was in the process of working his way upstream demanded that the stationary angler move. The stationary angler declared that the angler on the move should walk around him. The argument became more heated, ending only when the downstream angler picked up a rock the size of a softball and threw it in the water directly in front of the other angler—exactly where he had been casting to rising fish.

The angler on the move was in the wrong. He should never have thrown the rock. But, even before that, he should not have asked the stationary angler to move so he could continue upstream. He destroyed the fishing experiences of the other angler involved and those of us watching from across the water. He ruined his morning and his reputation. Anglers on every body of water make note of these situations, point to offenders, and repeat the tales over and over.

A COMMON MISTAKE

I heard a few guffaws when I insisted on including a section on stream etiquette, but it remains a necessary chapter until everyone practices proper etiquette on the stream.

It is a rare angler who has not witnessed or been a party to a squabble on the river. Granted, the shouting and actions of others do make for good tales in post-fishing reflections, but the discomfort they cause anglers while on the stream can ruin a fine day of fishing.

THE FIX

Stream etiquette is simply respect: respect for your fellow anglers, for the fish, for the land and landowners, for the environment. It is basically the Golden Rule (do unto others) with some added common sense.

Some states post streams with a Code of Stream Etiquette. For those that don't, this is a refresher course offering a few simple suggestions for when you aren't sure what to do.

ACCESS TO THE WATER

Unless granted an exemption, you are required to have a fishing license to fish most freshwater. The costs are set by the state, so please don't complain to the store selling the license. They receive a small payment, if any, for providing this service.

Pick up the state fishing regulations when you buy a license. Read them, and familiarize yourself with local fishing rules and regulations before getting on the water.

Make sure you have legal access to the waterway you intend to fish. This means either entering at a public access point, or having permission from a private landowner to enter on his land. Some states have fishing right-of-ways when streams run through private land, whereas others leave access strictly up to the landowner.

If you are entering at a public access site, observe the posted rules and regulations.

Ask permission of landowners before crossing private property, whether it's posted or not.

Observe local rules and regulations.

If you have your eye on private land, knock on the door of the nearby house. If there isn't one, go someplace else to fish. Respect the rights of the landowners:

- Park carefully. Watch for lawns or sensitive areas.
- Take care crossing fences. Fencing is expensive.
- Close all gates you have opened.
- Do not cross crop lands or damage crops.
- Always take time to talk with landowners if they come to you.
- Help a landowner whenever possible. Fifteen minutes of your time goes a long way.
- More than anything, landowners want to know who is on their property. Respect that.
- Remember that on the water, everyone is watching. Set a good example.
- And if you get permission to cross someone's land, don't show up with five friends in tow.

GETTING TO THE WATER

When walking down a path behind another angler, always alert the person you are following.

When you see someone already on the water, a wave of acknowledgment is all that is needed. Some anglers prefer to be left alone and not spoken to.

ON THE WATER

Keep noise to a minimum. Don't shout across the water to your fishing buddy. It is natural to get excited about hooking a large trout, and some anglers scream and yell to celebrate. These antics should be kept to a minimum out of respect for the stream and other anglers sharing it. Most of us are on the water to enjoy the quiet of a soft-flowing trout stream: the sound of the water, the birds singing, the breeze sweeping through the trees, and, best of all, the slurp of a large feeding trout.

Give other anglers room to fish. Keep at least thirty yards away from another angler on the larger pools and runs, or wait until they have passed you.

When choosing a fishing spot, always look upstream and downstream for other anglers.

If you are working your way downstream and you come upon an angler moving upstream, yield the right of way to the angler working upstream. Get out of the water and let him pass by, or just stop and pull your line in until he has moved above you.

Don't claim a productive fishing area by leaving your gear on the banks or planting your net in the mud and stepping away. Conversely, look at the banks to see if an angler is resting a spot before moving into the water. An angler resting fish still has the rights to that water.

If your favorite fishing spot is occupied, stop and watch the angler from a distance. Perhaps he is moving on, and you can take over the pool. Do not get into the water, though. The angler who was there first has the right of way. If you really want a particular spot, get up earlier.

On the other hand, if you aren't sure which direction an angler is going, it's best to ask. Sometimes anglers move upstream fishing the near side of a particular pool and, when they reach the top, plan to fish a current on the far side downstream. Don't ruin their day. You wouldn't want to have to change your plans if you had been the first angler on the stream.

Small streams are best fished working upstream. Most of the time, an angler won't mind someone following him as he fishes upstream. Follow these simple rules to improve your fishing day and his:

- Leave the lead angler plenty of room before you step into the water downstream.
- If you find that he is moving much more slowly than you, get out of the water to pass upstream. Tell the angler your plans. If you know the river, let him know where you plan to put into the river again.
- A considerate rule of thumb is to leave the angler an hour's worth of fishing before he reaches your upstream put-in site. In other words, he should be able to fish and move upstream at the pace he had been moving for an hour before reaching the section where you started fishing.
- If you find you are fishing behind another angler, your best option is to try another section of the stream. It will probably be more productive and infinitely more enjoyable for you.

When you are moving up or downstream to a new section, get out of the water and walk the paths wherever possible, so you don't disturb the water for those already fishing.

- Fish are very sensitive to vibrations and motion. If you can, choose paths that are farther away from the water's edge.
- When you see an angler fishing against the bank, give him plenty of room.
- If the situation is the reverse, and you are fishing the bank when someone walks up and asks "How's the fishing?" you may be tempted to say "It was fine before you showed up." Swallow that response. If you can free yourself from any anger, you may be able to point out some etiquette to an inexperienced angler or a total bozo.
- Verbal and even physical conflicts result in a negative experience for everyone.

Do get out of the water or step out of the path of an angler who is moving downstream while fighting a big fish on his line. You would expect the same courtesy when the fish is on your line.

The angler closest to the snag should untangle the lines.

When you visit a new area, you need to learn the basic rules of etiquette for the local water. You may be used to fishing quiet streams that aren't over-populated with anglers, but when you travel elsewhere, you should be prepared.

If you are fishing crowded waters and get your line tangled with another angler, the angler closest to the snag should reel in and untangle the lines, if possible.

The angler farther away should release line to allow for this. Communicate first! If the snag is too difficult to untangle, cut your leader so the other angler can reel in his line.

The same rules of etiquette should be followed when you are fishing from a boat. If you are entering the water at a public access site, anglers loading and unloading should do so quickly, as the sites tend to get crowded.

The angler who was on the water first has the right of way whether he is fishing or resting the water when you arrive.

The angler farther away should let out line.

When you are floating and come across wading anglers, stop fishing and reel in your line until you have passed their water.

If you are the wader, try to communicate to the boat where you are fishing, or which side you would prefer that the boat should pass you.

The boat must remember that the wader has less maneuverability than those floating and try to give the people in the water the widest berth possible.

FISHING WITH FRIENDS

Wading

If you are fishing with a buddy, the best approach is often to take turns—particularly if the stream is too small to accommodate both anglers at the same time.

If you are onto fish and have caught one or a few of good size, step aside and let your friend have your water. At the end of the day, it feels much better to leave knowing that you could have caught more fish than that you have hooked everything in the pool.

Or let your friend have first choice of fishing spot at the next pool.

Don't make fun of another angler's mistakes. And don't take advantage of him by casting to someone's rising fish after he has missed a strike. On a fishing trip with friends, I was once working a rising fish that kept refusing my flies. When I went to change my fly, I noticed my friend casting to the rise while I was tying on the new fly. Even though he didn't get the fish (and I eventually did), I never forgot the transgression.

If you don't have a productive day fishing, don't blame your equipment or position on the water. It doesn't sound reasonable, and no one wants to hear it.

Fishing from a Drift Boat

When fishing from a boat, it is often wise to establish a few ground rules before you get on the water:

- Use the oarlocks as your boundary: The angler in the bow casts in front of the boat and lets his fly drift back only until it is even with the oarlocks, while the angler in the stern of the boat casts only as far forward as the imaginary line running through the oarlocks to shore on both sides of the boat.

- Set a schedule for trading positions within the boat.
- Relinquish the bow if you are there and have caught a lot.
- Practice your casting before you float. And cast to the perfect spot on the bank under the bushes only if you are sure of your casting ability. Don't make your guide haul the boat back upstream to free your fly or risk having a snagged line zing through the air and hit someone after it snaps free.

RESPECT FOR THE FISH

Fish don't belong to us. They belong to the river. If you must take fish, try to take only hatchery fish, and release wild fish. Properly releasing a fish unharmed begins when you hook it.

- Use barbless hooks.
- Use the rod to fight the fish, always applying pressure opposite the direction the fish is moving.
- Use the strongest tippet possible, and land your fish quickly.

Nets with a catch-and-release bag help preserve the protective coating of a fish.
Photo credit: John Bonasera

- A landing net with a soft mesh bag is essential to landing large fish without harm.
- Keep a fish under the water while removing the hook.
- If you want to take a picture, get everything ready before lifting the fish out of the water.
- Consider limiting your catch. In spite of all our efforts to carefully release fish unharmed, some of them will die.

Fish only in ideal conditions for the fish. When the water is too warm and there is not enough oxygen in the stream, the fish are stressed and shouldn't be caught and played.

- Before casting to a fish in this situation, ask yourself whether it's really ethical to go for such a vulnerable fish.
- If you come across fish nosing into a cool feeder stream in the warm summer, consider going hiking instead of fishing.

Spawning takes a lot out of fish, and the last thing they need is to be caught and stressed further by an angler. If you're lucky enough to spot a fish guarding a redd (spawning bed), take some time to observe the sight, and then leave the fish in peace. Consider it doing your part to help repopulate the stream for future fishing seasons.

RESPECT THE ENVIRONMENT

- No one needs to tell you not to litter, but also be on the lookout for other people's trash.
- When finished with a leader, cut it into little bits and throw in a trashcan or bring it home for disposal.
- Designate a vest pocket for your trash, but don't forget to empty it periodically.
- Don't frighten livestock or wild animals that you may pass.

CARING FOR YOUR GEAR

A fly fisherman was taking his fourteen-year-old grandson on a fishing trip, the second in what he hoped would become a longstanding annual tradition for the two of them. We met in the morning at the fly shop, so that they could buy fishing licenses for the weekend. Mustering all his patience, the grandfather waited while his grandson tried on all the sunglasses on the rack and fingered the rods standing in the case. Next, the grandfather took the boy to the deli down the street for a can of soda. We reached the water, and the two of them began to dress for fishing while I prepared their rods. Last year, the older man had outfitted his grandson with a new set of bootfoot waders and his own rod and reel outfit. The boy's mother had packed everything up for his trip.

The boy put one foot into his waders and pulled it out with a shout. He claimed the boot was full of water. I picked up the waders and turned them over, emptying two boots of water onto the grass. It seems that the grandson had fallen into the river while fishing the year before and had never emptied the waders of water.

The two did make it to the water that day, but only after we returned to the fly shop to borrow a set of small waders.

A credible tale about a fourteen-year-old, but I have seen the same thing happen to a forty-one-year-old. It happens.

A COMMON PROBLEM

"The last time I went fishing was _____ ." In the autumn, or the spring, or summer. Maybe it was in the mountains or on a small stream or a lake. Fill in the blank. Whatever it is, it was most likely a different season or environment or water than the current one.

This is a universal excuse anglers make for not having the right gear with them or their equipment in order. It may have been that the angler was fishing in the late autumn and had removed the box of spring flies from his vest, and now here he was on the river for spring fishing without the right fly box. It may have been that he had fallen in the water and put away his wet waders without drying them first.

THE FIX

Fly fishing gear is not high tech. It doesn't clean itself, repair itself, or even freshen up over the winter. Chances are your equipment will be found on opening day exactly where you left it in the autumn and in the exact same condition. To avoid this, take care of your gear at the end of the season, so that it will be ready to fish in the spring.

A few important projects to maintain your fly fishing equipment are described in the list below. Use this as a checklist for the end of the season, or make your own.

ROD TUBES AND BAGS

Make sure that all of the caps to your rod tubes are open, allowing fresh air to clear out the moisture that may have been trapped inside the tubes during the fishing season.

> ### GUIDE TIP
> Tape the rod cap to the tube to ensure finding it again in a couple of months.

Inspect the rod bags or socks for wear. Rods tend to poke holes through the bottom of socks. Repair any holes, so that the rod is completely protected the next time you take it fishing.

RODS

Check your rods for nicks or scratches, which can become weak spots that eventually cause the rod to break. If you notice nicks, consult with the rod manufacturer about the best protective care.

This is the perfect time to clean your rod. Wipe it down with a damp cloth to clean away any residue dirt or pond scum from the last use.

Your grip may have darkened with use, or the cork may have become rough. An easy way to clean your grip is to use Lava soap. This bar soap has a gentle abrasive ingredient that feels like sand particles. Wet the soap, and rub it all around the handle. If you cannot find Lava soap, use a mild soap such as Ivory and a glove or sponge specifically for exfoliating. These are available at local drug stores. Put a little water on the glove, and soap it up. The cork grip will be free of hand oils and dirt. It will feel better to your hand and will last a lot longer with this care.

Be careful not to use too much water. You don't want to soak the reel seat and cause the wood to swell or the glue to loosen up. And don't use a heavy abrasive or you may change the shape of your grip.

REELS

For the most part, reels are sturdy mechanisms that need little upkeep. Give a few turns to the reel, winding in both directions to check for dirt inside the gear mechanism. If you hear a grinding noise or feel resistance, take off the spool (if possible) or open the reel and remove any sand that may be trapped inside.

Wipe off the reel, but be careful around the gear mechanism so that you don't wipe away the oil that keeps it working smoothly. Inspect the grease for any sand particles and remove stones if you find them. If the reel needs it, add a drop or two of gear oil to the mechanism.

LINES

Clean your lines. Take the line off the reel and put it in a sink full of water. Swirl the water around to loosen any sand. Dry the line, and run it through a line cleaner pad. This job requires extreme patience, if only to avoid creating a snarl of a long length of fly line.

GUIDE TIP

Coil the fly line loosely, and hang it over the neck of a hanger for the winter. This helps eliminate tight memory coils from your line.

If your line is well-used, check carefully for cuts and abrasions, which can affect the utility of your line: Floating lines can take on water and sink; sinking lines may drop too fast.

LEADER

Replace your leader for the new season. If you buy tapered leaders, it's a simple matter to pull a new one out of the packet and put it on your line. If you build your leaders, replace the butt section, or at least check the knots for dirt or cuts. A fresh leader is the best way to start the new season—no knots or crimps to hamper your presentation.

FLIES

The off-season is the time of year when tyers replenish their boxes with newly tied flies. You can also refurbish the ones that got you through the last season.

Straighten the flies in your boxes using whatever system or non-system you have. Organize your fly boxes by season, type of fly (dry, emerger, nymph, etc.), or river—whatever works for you. Take inventory of what you have and what you need.

Sharpen hooks. Use a needle to clear the hook eyes of knots or head cement.

Freshen up the dry flies that are matted down by steaming them with a steamer or over a pot of boiling water. Let the flies dry standing upright hooked into a foam box. Make sure they have dried completely before putting them away. Space your dry flies well in the box, so that they are not crushed for the rest of the winter.

WADERS

Did you have water in your waders during the season? Did you fish anyway? Now is the time to patch those leaks. There are many ways to find a leak.

Try shining a flashlight from the inside of the waders when you stand in a dark room. If you see a pinprick of light, you have found your hole.

If you have stockingfoot waders, you can try running a hose in them, turning on the water and watching for it to begin seeping out. Look closely because the hole may be very small and allow only a small drip of water to seep out.

My favorite method for finding a leak in waders is to coat the outside with a layer of liquid soap and blow air down the inside using a vacuum hose or blowdryer. A bubble should appear where the hole is in the fabric. Mark the hole and then clean the outside of your waders. Make sure you get all the soap off before you use them again, so you don't pollute the river. Also remember that a blowdryer needs plenty of intake air to counter overheating, so plan this project carefully.

Check the soles of your boots to make sure that your felt is secure and thick. If you have non-felt soles, look for wear, especially in the toe area. Tighten studs on your boots and replace any that have been lost during the season.

FISHING VEST

Anglers who are not superstitious about doing this should clean their empty vests in a washing machine. A fresh vest is a great way to start the next season.

Whether or not it gets washed, your vest could probably use a little organizing. Check pockets for snippets of tippet or other garbage.

Wear your vest as you go through the pockets. This will help remind you of how it's been organized. If you find yourself rearranging the contents of your pockets, you will appreciate knowing whether or not the gear will fit comfortably in new pockets when you have the vest on.

While you are rummaging through your vest, check the quantities of floatant, strike indicators, tippet material, split-shot, and everything else you carry. If you have several partially filled bottles of floatant, stand two opened containers one on top of another with one upside down to fill the bottom bottle. If you need new split-shot, remember not to buy lead.

GEAR BAG

Straighten your gear bag and eliminate any extras you don't need, such as four flashlights. If you keep a change of clothing in the bag all winter, trade it for a fresh set. Replenish your bug spray and sunscreen.

AQUATIC INVASIVE SPECIES

An unfortunate effect of anglers traveling to different bodies of water to fish is the spread of aquatic invasive species. Many fishing areas have enacted regulations in an effort to stem the further spread of invasive species. You can take measures as well.

One of the most notorious of the aquatic invasive species is Didymo. A freshwater form of algae found in cold, flowing streams, Didymo is an organism that can smother the natural plant life and organisms in a river, altering the habitat and ruining the ecosystem of the stream.

Didymo can be carried easily by anglers from one water system to the next. As we are well aware, felt soles and boats are the usual suspects for tracking invasive species into otherwise clean water. But, the Didymo cells can also be carried on clothing, waders, flies, fishing lines—anything that stays wet after a dunk in infested water.

SOLUTIONS

- Wearing non-felt sole boots will reduce the chances of carrying organisms from one water system to another.
- Dry out and clean all gear and clothing.
- Felt-sole boots, waders, and equipment can be cleaned of Didymo with several solutions including bleach (which is hard on your gear); hot water (which is hard on Gore-Tex); and salt.

GUIDE TIP

I carry a bucket and salt in my car to soak my boots at the end of the fishing day: five parts water to one part salt.

Allowing gear to dry thoroughly will kill Didymo as well, but we all know how long it takes to dry felt soles completely. Anglers planning to enter a different river with slightly damp soles risk carrying the organism with them.

Those fortunate to have a collection of wading boots can also designate a different pair for each stream fished regularly.

ACKNOWLEDGMENTS

I did not learn to fish by myself. Nor did I write this book alone. A heartfelt bow to Nick Lyons, who encouraged me to write. His support and an envelope full of my articles edited by Nick are cherished gifts.

Before there was writing, there was fishing. I thank my parents for putting a rod in my hand at the age of three and for letting me fish all these years since. Thanks to my first fishing buddy, my sister Emily. She sat in a rowboat with me for hours and hours, but I think she really came along for the fruit pies. And to everyone I've ever fished with. You have each taught me something.

I have been fortunate to learn from the best: Nancy Zakon, thank you for entrusting your Julianas to me; Joan Wulff, you are an inspiration and a friend; Bob Jacklin, the smoothest cast in the west, fishing with you is always an honor; Floyd Franke, thank you, my friend, for your encouragement and some of my favorite clients; and Bert Darrow, you improved my fishing and taught me how to approach the river as a guide.

I am deeply indebted to Karen Kaplan for her support and insightful comments at each stage of this project. From her first day on Long Pond when she bested me with the purple rubber worm to last weekend when we traded flies on the Farmington, she has been subjected to my guidelines for years.

I have enjoyed writing this book, thanks to Jay Cassell, who pushed and prodded and smiled and suggested—all at the right times. Thank you, Jay, for making it come true.

Even without words, there are pictures. Each one tells a story to the reader and evokes a memory. My gratitude and smiles to the photographers and anglers who offered their images:

John Bonasera, Tony Bonavist, Shannon Brightman, Joseph Ceballos, Bob Chilton, Bert Darrow, Patsy Dreher, Dort Giordino, Keith Godfrey, Irene Huhner, Kurt Huhner, Karen Kaplan, Maurice Mahler, Henry McVickar, Lansing McVickar, Michelle O'Dea, Sandye Renz, Mary Rolland, Kat Rollin, Randy Thomas, Charles Warner, Marcelo Widman. And cheers to those anglers and guides whose pictures illuminated my words: Edward Boland, Julia Bradford, Hamp Cross, Alan Dreher, Jeremy Kehrein, David Kramer, Donna Tate McDonald, Pat Piccione, Len Pickard, Karen Poulter, Brian Purcell, David Purcell, Elizabeth Shapiro, Tommy Sherman, Fred Shulman, Margaret Tate.

I offer a round of applause to Rod Walinchus, whose illustrations bring words to life, and Constance Renfrow, whose publishing and computer knowledge saved me many times.

INDEX

NOTES